The Decoratin Of Metals: Chasing, Repoussé And Sawpiercing...

John Harrison

Dorothy [illegible]

2/9/62

THE DECORATION OF METALS

MODERN REPOUSSÉ.

From the "Pompeian Lady" Plaque, by MOREL LADEUIL.

[*See page* 76.

THE

DECORATION OF METALS

CHASING, REPOUSSÉ AND SAW PIERCING

BY

JOHN HARRISON

[illegible]

[illegible] AND MODELLER

WITH 180 ILLUSTRATIONS OF WORKS BY VARIOUS ARTISTS
AND ORIGINAL DESIGNS

London—CHAPMAN & HALL, Ltd.

THE

DECORATION OF METALS

CHASING, REPOUSSÉ AND SAW-PIERCING

BY

JOHN HARRISON

(*Late with Messrs. Elkington & Co.*)

WORKER IN REPOUSSÉ, CHASER, DESIGNER, AND MODELLER

WITH 180 ILLUSTRATIONS OF WORKS BY VARIOUS ARTISTS AND ORIGINAL DESIGNS

LONDON—CHAPMAN & HALL, LTD.

1894

PREFACE.

ALTHOUGH numerous works have been written upon metals and their respective uses, and short descriptions of the various methods of decoration given in Digby Wyatt's comprehensive publication "*Metal Work and its Artistic Design*," no attempt, to my knowledge, has hitherto been made by a professional worker engaged in the decoration of metals to assist the teacher and student alike in the art, by placing before them in book form a course of lessons comprising technical information and designs in progressive form which are calculated to be best suited for the articles they are intended to decorate.

I believe, with the rapid increase of technical schools throughout the United Kingdom, that such a book is greatly needed which can give to those interested in acquiring this art of decoration every information of methods practised in the workshop, and showing, so far as a book can, the most legitimate means of acquiring good results. The decoration of metals has not been with me an amateur hobby, but a professional means of subsistence for more than twenty years, and that my long experience may prove of real help to the student is the earnest desire of the author.

June, 1894.

CONTENTS.

CHAPTER V.

CHAPTER VI.

CHAPTER VII.

CHAPTER VIII.

CHAPTER IX.

CHAPTER X.

CHAPTER XI.

CHAPTER XII.

CHAPTER XIII.

LIST OF ILLUSTRATIONS.

CHAPTER I.

CHAPTER II.

CHAPTER III.

CHAPTER IV.

CHAPTER V.

CHAPTER VI.

CHAPTER VII.

CHAPTER VIII.

CHAPTER IX.

CHAPTER X.

Saw-Piercing.

CHAPTER XI.

Flat Chasing.

CHAPTER XII.

Flat Chasing.

CHAPTER XIII.

FLUTING.

INTRODUCTION.

THE rapidly increasing love for artistic work in metals, may be observed by the establishing of annual exhibitions in connection with the "Arts and Crafts," and "Armourers'" Institutions; and by the erection of technical schools throughout the United Kingdom. It is doubtful if these schools will accomplish all their aims; but one thing, I think, is beyond ambiguity—that of extending a knowledge of metal work hitherto unpossessed, and infusing into the earnest student an ambition to accomplish such really good and artistic specimens that he is excluded from doing in the ordinary commercial workshop. That he or she will not only be able to distinguish the truly beautiful from the inartistic and vulgar—but will place a proportionate value upon them.

Not very long ago I was asked by a manufacturer for some brass plates for the fronts of bellows. I submitted several different designs in repoussé, upon which the manufacturer at once fetched a stamped design, which of course would be accomplished by one blow from the stamp-hammer, a purely mechanical process. He placed it by the side of mine—which had necessitated some hundreds of blows of varied strength—and remarked that he bought the stamped one for the same price that I asked for mine, and it *looked* so much more than mine —meaning that there was a greater amount of ornament upon it. "But surely," I remarked, "you do not expect the same quantity of ornament executed by hand for the same money that you buy a stamping which is the result of one blow?" "But," said he, "our customers do not understand the difference of the work—and I fear the one in hand repoussé would have little sale compared with the stamped one." We cannot attach any blame to the manufacturer; still, this same man was the possessor of several paintings, and although by artists of no great reputation, yet had the smallest of these works been asked for in exchange for a hundred lithographs or oleographs—or any other mechanical productions of the kind—such a request had been laughed at as ridiculous and absurd. I should consider it highly improbable too, that a painter has ever been asked by a dealer to produce him something similar for 50*s*. that he has just asked 50*l*. for. And yet this is not a very uncommon occurrence in the case of artistic metal work and manufacturing. Their prices are restricted, and it is only such a firm of silversmiths as Messrs. Elkington & Co., who pay unlimited sums for artistic metal work—and I very much doubt if it is nearly so profitable (in a financial sense) as the every-day selling productions, even to this great firm.

In the sixteenth and seventeenth centuries the goldsmith's art was, to a great extent, held in the same esteem as the painter and sculptor's. Although this difference—too palpable—then, as now, existed, viz., the omission of any signature on a large number of the most beautiful of the goldsmith's productions, while the work of the painter and sculptor are very rarely without one. And students and lovers of artistic metal work have to content themselves to-day with the name of the country, article, and supposed date, in many instances, when reviewing the glorious results of the patient, and, no doubt, loving labours of those great souls of the past. This omission, truly, steals no beauty from works thus handed down to us; but it arouses an interest in us to know those men of two and three centuries ago who worked so earnestly, so truthfully in their day that their honesty of purpose has proved a beauty from then through all men's days until it has reached us, to be a charming delight to our own—supplying as they do our art galleries and museums with perpetual feasts for the minds of millions.

That good work in metal, as good as at any period of the world's existence, is executed to-day is beyond doubt, and as proof of this we have only to turn to the productions by the famous Vechte and his helper Morel-Ladeuil, and to hundreds of specimens that bear no signatures; and that idea, so blindly fostered by the worshippers of the past, that the workmen of to-day are far inferior to our forefathers, is as erroneous as it is unjust. We have but to examine the setting of gems in the better class of jewellery; the mountings, and general workmanship in works in silver, copper, brass, or other metals; the unsurpassed, perhaps unequalled, damascening by our Asiatic friends, the Japanese, to convince us that the present century can boast artists equal to those of any former period. But the seeds of commerce have been scattered broadcast, that even the Land of the Sun has not escaped, and the products of the truly beautiful afford not sufficient nutrition for those honest sowers, who nurtured the fruit to subsist upon; hence the ardent zeal for the latter is not unfrequently starved, until it takes refuge in its despair by feeding and fattening upon the former. Our ancestors, however, made the articles in most instances as well as decorated them, while the decorator of to-day, in ninety-nine cases out of every hundred, decorates only, and in many cases designs not the ornament he so skilfully executes. Even the Amazon Dish by Vechte, which is perhaps as fine a specimen of repoussé that has ever been accomplished, was designed by the celebrated sculptor Jean Feuchere, his fellow-countryman.

We owe this change in the method of working to the introduction of machinery, and the division of the silversmith or metal workers' trade into many branches, and by this means a rapidity of production, which embraces perfection of workmanship, is achieved; e.g., the cup on page 87, and which was "manufactured to price," passed through the hands of fifteen different workmen and one workwoman. Many shapes are spun now in brass, copper, silver, and even German silver—a very hard metal—which even twenty years ago were hammered into shape. Hence it will readily be understood, that an ornamenter is now satisfied to obtain from a spinner or hammerer, or both, the shape he is about to decorate which, if he undertook to form himself, would entail greater time and labour, with a less satisfactory result. Such a change is, of course, only the natural outcome of the general progress of the age; but the commercial spirit which permeates all labour has not permitted art to escape; and in woodwork, pottery, and metal, it pierces to the very core like (to use a simile that has grown somewhat musty) a grub in a ripe pear.

It was remarked by a silversmith quite recently, that he should help the technical schools all he could, as they would soon produce a multitude of workmen, when he should get his goods ornamented at a much cheaper rate than he was then paying. We trust that he will prove as false in his prophecy as he has proved false in his love for art; and that such a selfish end will be thwarted by the additional knowledge acquired, and that every work of artistic merit, in wood, pottery, or metal, shall bear the artist's name with the date inscribed upon it, and be esteemed with the same significance as the signature of a painter or sculptor.

With all the painful knowlege of false helpers before

us, it is, however, encouraging to know that we have the earnest and true, in Herkomer, Ruskin, and others of like natures; that we may foster the hope of a time being not very far distant when the art workers in every branch of industry, who beautify our homes, will receive the respect, or even reverence, that they have long merited; when the works that have been achieved by hammer and punch shall be viewed with the same eager interest as those wrought upon the canvas with colour and brush. To-day we may ask, "Who are these men? What are they? Are their declining years—when their hands shall lose their cunning—secured against poverty by the State?" To the two first questions the answer may be: We only know their works. And to the last: Not yet!

However, in the present volume, it is my intention to give all the practical help I can to the student in repoussé, chasing, and saw-piercing in combination with the two former, leaving modelling, etching, damascening, enamelling, engraving, and niello for a future volume. In such a work, I am of necessity obliged to omit many very beautiful specimens by workmen of the present as well as of the past. At the same time I have endeavoured to place before the student examples photographed from the actual works, and original designs, that I think best suited for the articles they are intended to decorate, starting with the very simplest and making them progressive. And although good masters and good books can greatly facilitate the advancement of students; can help them out of difficulties; can aid them in doing good work, they can never make good workmen or workwomen of them, the *making* is in her or his own keeping—where it exists at all. This cannot be too strongly borne in mind; for when a pupil is placed under a good master it is too often thought that his or her aim is half accomplished.

Again, every student should endeavour to become a designer, and model in clay or wax the design he or she is about to convey to the metal. It will prevent indirect working, give a conception of the result and a readier means of gaining a good one. In the first case a bad design can never be made pleasing to the sense of sight, however well it may be executed; and in support of this I would remark that very recently I saw at an art exhibition in London a design for a carpet that had the appearance of an intricate meshwork of wires and strings ready to entrap every foot that ventured upon it and throw the venturer down. And for the second—the modelling first in clay or wax—it aids the student to combine good work with a design, and if both are good the success aimed at must be complete. On the other hand, if a good and suitable design be worked out indifferently, it will convey, in the majority of instances, an amount of pleasure to the beholder. Take, for instance, the subject of pictures. How many, indifferent in technique, have touched the heart of the multitude by the pathos the ideas in them have conveyed? To assist the student in the principles of design, I know no better book than Mr. F. G. Jackson's "Lessons on Decorative Design," a text-book of principles and practice, and which cannot be too highly recommended. It is a thoroughly practical work by a thoroughly practical artist.

THE DECORATION OF METALS.

CHASING, REPOUSSÉ AND SAW-PIERCING.

CHAPTER I.

CHASING AND REPOUSSÉ.

CHASING is a means of working out flat applied designs on gold, silver, and inexpensive metals with small punches, about four inches long, very much resembling old nails on first sight, but which, on close inspection, are found to have variously shaped ends for the convenience of working out with clearness the many different designs they are used for. (See Illustrations Nos. 1, 2, 3, 4, 5, 6, 7, 8, 9, 10, 11, and 12.)

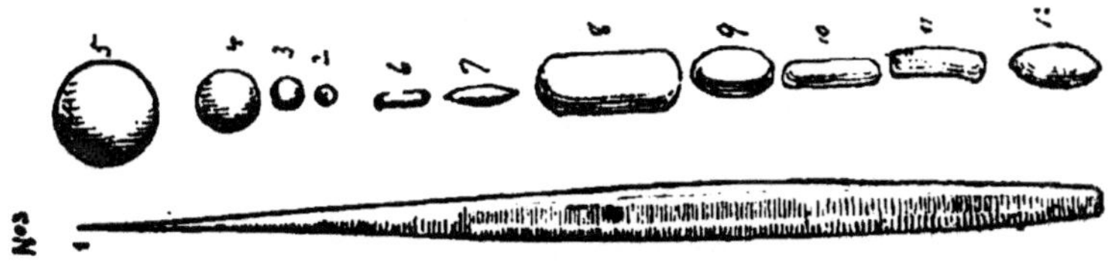

Repoussé is a French term applied to raised ornament, obtained by similar means, and with similar punches.

When designs in repoussé are worked upon articles that are comparatively flat—such as salvers, shields,

PLATE I.

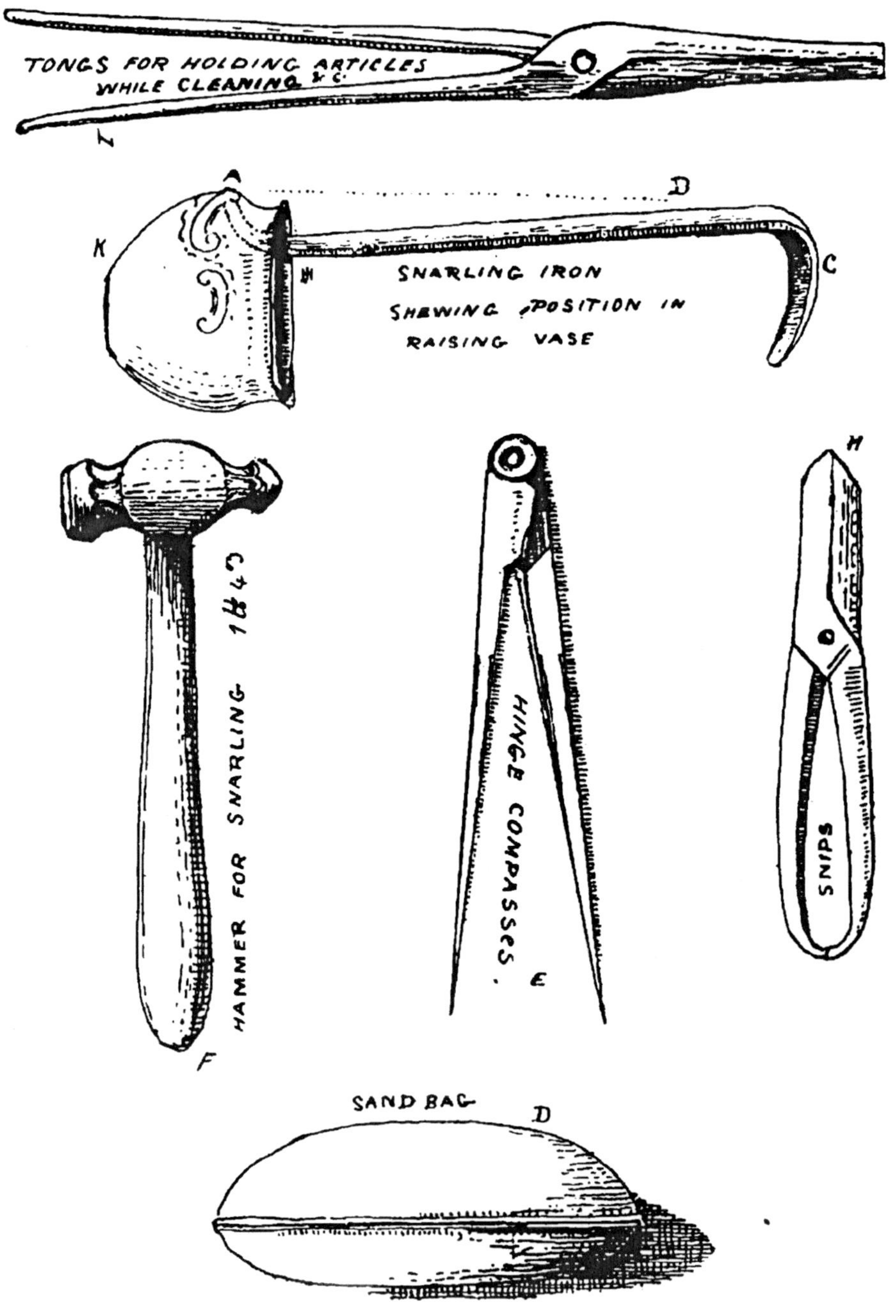
TONGS FOR HOLDING ARTICLES WHILE CLEANING &c.
A
D
K
C
SNARLING IRON SHEWING POSITION IN RAISING VASE
H
HAMMER FOR SNARLING
F
HINGE COMPASSES.
E
SNIPS
SAND BAG
D

PLATE II.

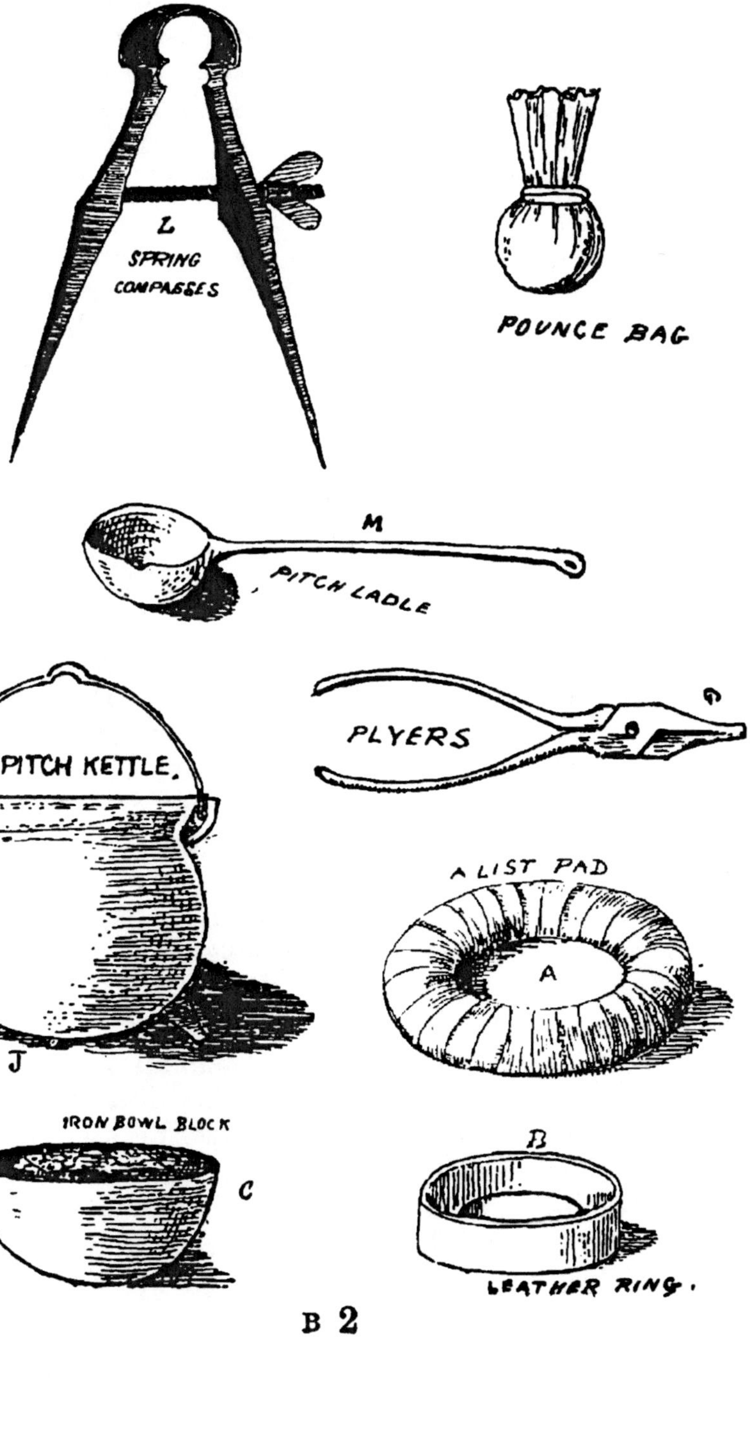
L
SPRING
COMPASSES
POUNCE BAG
M
PITCH LADLE
PLYERS
PITCH KETTLE.
J
A LIST PAD
A
IRON BOWL BLOCK
C
B
LEATHER RING.

door-plates, or any article that has a back easily accessible—it is beaten up with a punch held by the hand. If the article be quite flat, as in the case of a door-plate, it is usual to stick it face downwards upon a block of hard wood about two inches, or a slab of stone one and a half inches thick, which is first coated with a hot liquid mixture of pitch and plaster of Paris of even proportions. The pure pitch is put first into a cast-iron gipsy-kettle (see J. on Plate II.) and watched carefully whilst heating to prevent it boiling over, owing to its inflammable nature. When the whole of the pitch is reduced to a liquid, the plaster of Paris is added by degrees, but great care should be taken to secure perfect dryness in the plaster, as the slightest damp in it will cause the pitch to boil over when it is added to it. It should also be stirred with an iron ladle (see Plate II.) until every particle of plaster has disappeared from sight. In summer-time it is usual to add a little more plaster than in winter, and in the latter season an addition of Russian tallow is not only very beneficial, but frequently quite requisite for the purpose of softening the cement, and thereby preventing, to an extent, the metal from springing from it; an addition of beeswax will also improve the cement by making it much more tenacious. It should be poured in the hot state with the ladle upon the block, to cover with a level coating more space than the metal will occupy. It will be sufficiently set in a minute or two, when a second coating should be added. The metal should then be greased on the side to be stuck on, and pressed quickly with the fingers and thumbs into the cement before it has had time to get hot through; the fingers can be removed, and two flat-ended mallets, or anything flat, that will not make indentations, used in place of them, pressing near the two ends of the metal until the cement has come slightly over it, for the better security of the sticking. It is now ready for working, and in the case of repoussé, for beating up while still warm; but for flat chasing or outlining on the front it should be allowed to cool first. There are, however, other means of raising besides sticking the work on to cemented blocks, viz., on sandbags, wood, wax—a mixture of beeswax and potato starch—and lead, when the metal is thin—*i.e.*, six or eight size in a Birmingham metal-gauge plate. Very good results can be obtained by these means; and very recently has come under my notice an ornamental dragon, some two feet square, that was raised in the first way, but it cannot be very successfully applied even to large specimens of flat metal, and in small ones it is quite impracticable because there is not sufficient resistance in the sandbag to retain a level ground. And, although lead and wood have greater resistance, they very soon get out of shape, and the result in beating up flat panels on sandbags or wood is not very satisfactory, and, indeed, the uplifting of the ground in the large specimen cited is very conspicuous; but the labour of laying it back (making the ground level) in such instances is greatly reduced by placing it on a flat anvil and tracing lightly round the outline of the ornament with blunt punches, such as Nos. 10 and 11, previous to sticking it on the cement to finish it from the front; the ornament, however, is never so firm and pronounced as when beaten on cement, and experts adopt this means. Boxwood punches and mallets with rounded ends may be successfully used for beating up large work. Nearly all the tools used for raising purposes are invariably blunt-faced ones and of a shape most suited to the formation of the ornament desired, although comparatively sharp ones may be used with advantage for lifting the edges of reeds, petals and suchlike. To hold the punches, either for chasing or repoussé, in a manner that will command their movements in the direction required for the formation of a design, is the first great and difficult task of the pupil. It must be grasped by the thumb and first finger of the left hand; the second finger is used to keep it in position, while the third is pressed firmly upon the article undergoing decoration, and serves to guide the punch with precision in parts requiring minute detail (see Fig. C); but where a long straight or curved line is needed, a better result is gained by keeping all the fingers off the metal (see Fig. D).

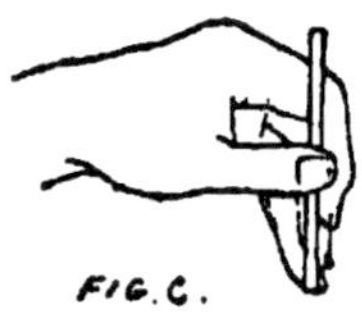

FIG. C.

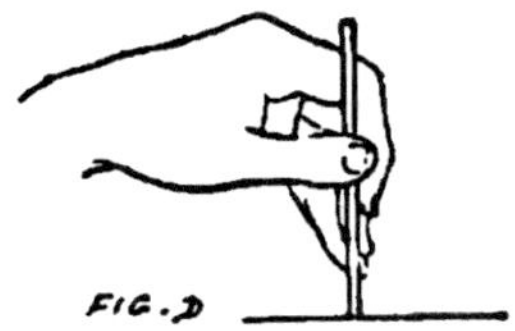

FIG. D

To avoid being misunderstood, however, I would remark here that the latter way can only be accomplished with advantage by those who have already had considerable experience. The hammer (Fig. 13) should be held by the right hand, the thick ovated end of the handle resting in the palm, and the forefinger resting upon the upper part (see Fig. B).

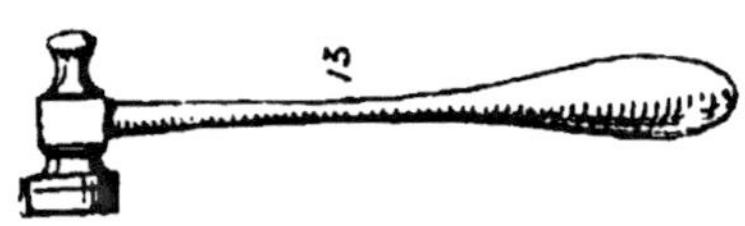

FIG. B

The first objects a teacher in any branch of art should always have in view are the simplest means of portraying his subject so as to make it, as early as possible, attractive, interesting, and instructive to the student; consistent, of course, with sound fundamental principles. It will, therefore, be our aim to lay before the student the very easiest forms of design, which require the least possible amount of practical knowledge to produce, but, when executed with care, will have a pleasing result, and may be put to use. Fig. 1 is drawn one-third full size—3×10½ inches.

The most suitable metal will be brass or copper, eight metal-gauge soft-rolled, and should be cut 11½ or 12 inches long by 4½ or 5 inches wide, to allow a

FIG. I.

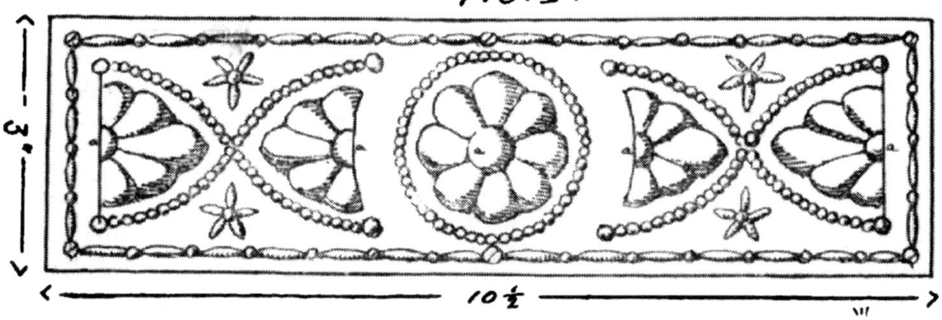

margin for the ornament. If it is cut the exact size required to be when finished, it will not only get out of shape while working, but will spring from the cement before the design is completed, and necessitate a second, or even a third or fourth sticking on, when one will

FIG. I.A

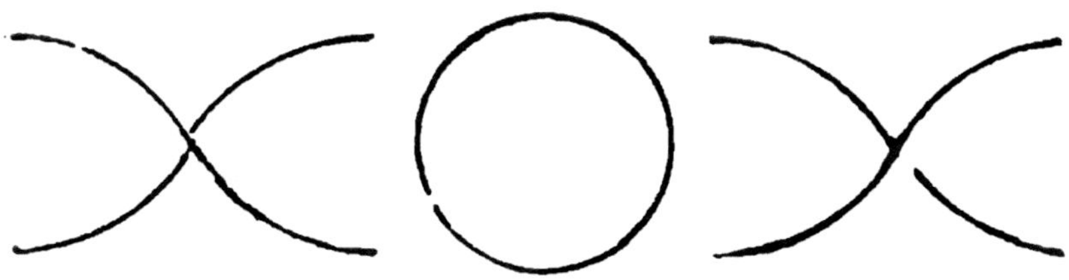

frequently serve the purpose. Before sticking it to the cemented block, it should be flattened with a boxwood mallet on an iron or steel anvil or smooth piece of thick, hard wood. A little finely powdered pumice mixed with oil, and rubbed on the surface with a piece of flannel or cotton waste, will (in the absence of a polishing lathe and Trent sand) make it sufficiently smooth to work upon. The ornament should then be scratched on with a pointed punch (see No. 1), and the metal afterwards greased and stuck on as described elsewhere. The lines of dots need not be marked as on Fig. 1, but as indicated on Fig. 1A. The largest portions of the ornament should be highest, and therefore, in this instance, the centre rosette and semi-rosettes should be beaten up first, while the pitch is in a warm and, therefore, soft state. Take No. 3 punch and hold it perfectly upright, and strike the five parts marked A, and then the sections, starting from them with No. 9. By the time this portion is finished the No. 2 punch may be used for the lines enclosing the rosettes, the dots in the border, and centres of stars; next, the elliptical-shaped tool, No. 7, for remainder of border; and last—being

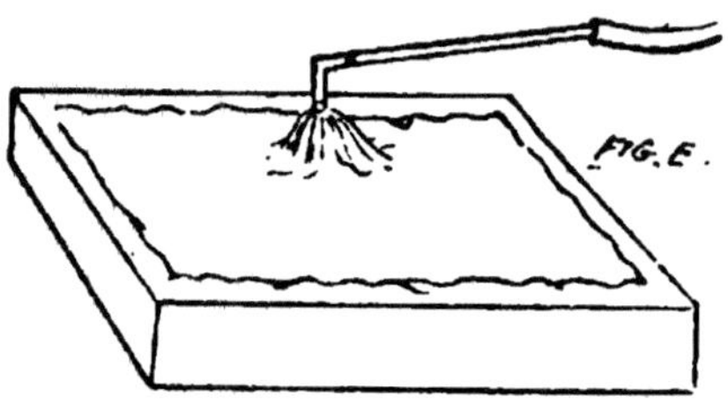

FIG. E.

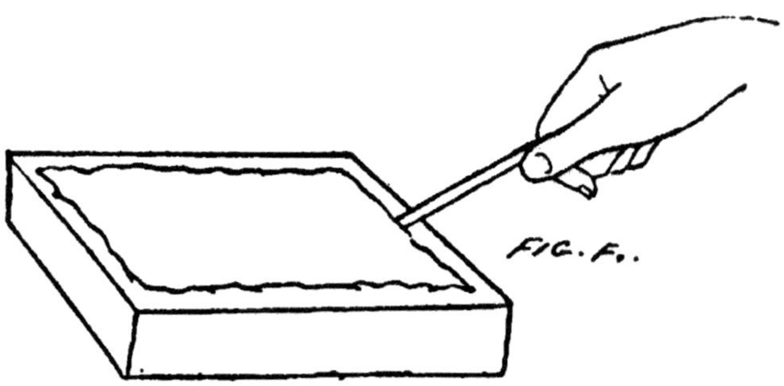

FIG. F.

the lightest or lowest in relief—the same tool for rays of stars should be used. Now that the work of ornamenting is finished, the gas should be applied, beginning at the corners and moving it slowly round (see Fig. E). A blow-lamp may be used with advantage, although an ordinary fishtail burner with a foot or eighteen inches of indiarubber piping (as shown in the above Fig.) attached to the gaspipes, will answer the purpose very well. A lever (a small screw driver, or some less expensive flat-shaped implement) should then be applied to the edges of the metal as soon as the pitch is sufficiently melted (see Fig. F.), and moved along to the fastened parts until the article is totally released. By holding it over the gas for a few seconds with a pair of small tongs or pliers, and then rubbing it with a little cotton waste dipped in clean oil, the dirty, sticky, opaque coating of oil—rendered so by its adhesion to the pitch—will readily be removed, and, if a little turps is afterwards applied with a small, hard brush, and the article dried out in fine box sawdust, it will be freed from grease and its cleanliness complete. This method of cleaning applies to all kinds of articles that are flat or nearly so —*i.e.*, trays, fruit baskets, plaques, and all such work that the hand can readily get at; but vessels that are too small in the mouth to admit the hand, such as vases, claret and cream jugs, should be immersed either into hot oil or a cleansing fluid prepared specially for this purpose by Messrs. Jeys, Aston, Birmingham, and by other chemists and drysalters. In the matter of punch bowls and very large vessels, it is more convenient to fill them with the fluid after the thickest portion of the pitch has been removed with oiled rag by the hand, as the coating is sometimes very thick, especially in the embossed parts. There are several methods, too, of getting the *bulk* of the pitch out of the articles last mentioned. A punchbowl being larger at the mouth than any other part, being wider than it is deep, and having no recesses to confine the cement, it may very readily be broken out by striking it sharply with the heavier hammer used for snarling several times a little from the centre; but the bowl should be held the while on the hand or with the hand and arm, because, if allowed to rest on anything that resists the blows, it will not only damage the work, but render the task of emptying almost impossible. This method would not, however, be a suitable one for ladies, and in the case of a lady student it were better to whiten the bowl, place it upside downwards, with its edge resting upon three bricks, and to apply the gas as in Fig. E until the bulk drops from it. In the case of a claret-jug, where the neck is invariably narrower than the body, it is customary to roast the pitch out of it in front of a sharp fire, coating it first with wet whiting to prevent reflection, and suspending it from a bottle-jack, or by ten or twelve thicknesses of worsted, secured at the top and bottom and twisted two or three times in the centre round a door-key, for the purpose of raising or lowering, as the heating may require. Another very effective means of removing the pitch is by roasting it out, as described in the next chapter.

CHAPTER II.

CHASING AND REPOUSSÉ.

WHEN a number of the articles are ready at one time for emptying the cement from them, the quickest means is by placing them in a gas-oven, about two feet square, fitted with atmospheric gas-burners round three sides near the bottom. A movable pan about four inches deep, and large enough to escape the flame of gas jets, is placed on the bottom of the oven to receive the melted pitch as it falls. The oven and pan are made of sheet iron.

The articles when ready to be emptied are bound with wire and suspended from rods near the top on hooks, which connect the article to the rod, or are placed upon movable rods which rest midway down on strips of sheet-iron. The strips are laid flat against the sides of the oven, to which they are riveted and then bent outwards and upwards, in which small incisions are made from end to end to receive the rods and keep them in position.

A gas blow-lamp may be used with great advantage to empty articles that are wider or nearly as wide at the mouth as at any other part, but it is a dangerous operation when applied to articles with small mouths or narrow necks and large bodies, for, if the greatest care is not taken, the accumulation of hot compressed air in the bodies created by heating those parts before there has been a vent through the neck or mouth will give rise to an explosion, which will seriously damage, if not spoil, the decorated articles, and will, in many instances, inflict great personal injury upon the one employed in emptying.

In Fig. II. the triangular-shaped pin-tray should be cut out in copper or brass, of six or eight-metal-gauge, the exact size required. The work not being very near to the edge, there is no need for a margin to be left, as in the case of the finger plate. The centre of the sunflower should first be raised, while warm, with a

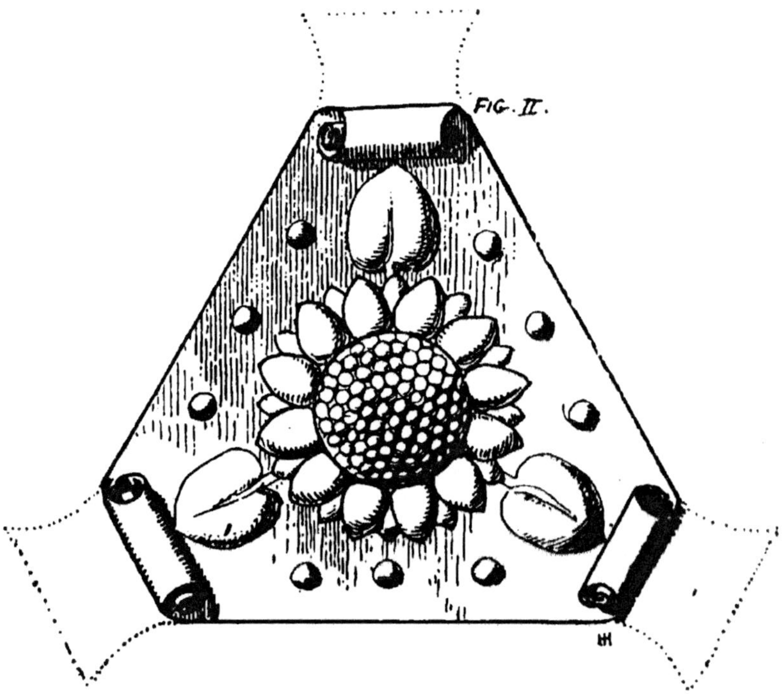

large round ball punch (No. 5). When a little cooler the three leaves and petals, with No. 9 punch, striking the leaves on each side and leaving the centres so as to give relief to them, but striking in the centres of the petals. The centre bead of the three at the sides struck next with No. 4 punch, and the others with No. 3, and last the seeds in the sunflower with Nos. 2 or 3. It can then be released and cleaned in the same way as the finger-plate, and afterwards the corners rolled in with a pair of pliers or small tongs with rounded parallel jaws from the dotted lines at the ends.

Fig. III. should be treated in the same way, the rosette and four long leaves shooting from it should be made highest in the centre. No. 8 tool should be used for them first, the centre and twelve large beads with No. 3; the small beads should be struck last with

FIG. III.

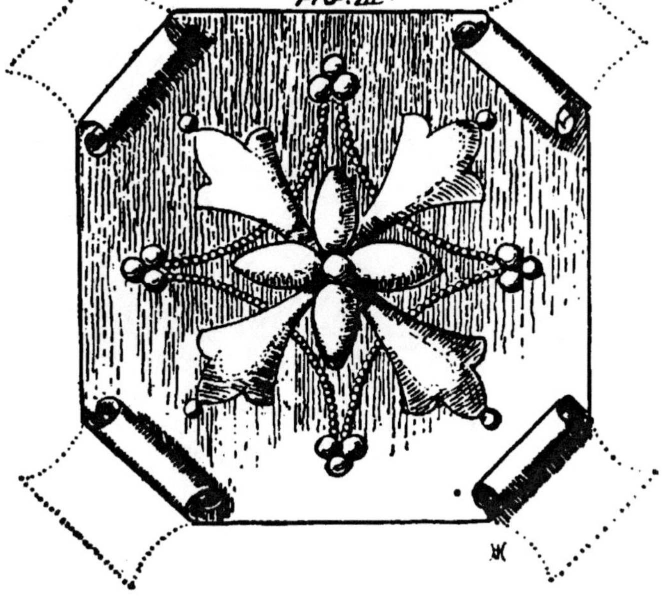

No. 2 punch when the work is cold, or very nearly so. This rule, to repeat what is specified in Chapter I., should always be adopted, viz., that of beating up the largest and boldest parts first, while the pitch is warm. It is a fruitless labour to attempt to beat up large masses on cold cement, unless very soft—which state unfits it for the smaller ornament; therefore, to avoid three or four, or even more stickings and disappointment, if the work becomes nearly cold before there has been time to complete the heaviest work, it is always advisable to re-warm it with the gas, or place it before a sharp fire. If you do not work quite close up to the outline of the ornament when warm, the space allowed will be lifted by beating the other parts, and the ground will remain comparatively even.

FIG. IV.

Fig. IV. (a round pin-tray) should be slightly greased inside and filled with the hot liquid cement, and allowed to set. It should then (while still warm) be stuck on a block with more melted cement, and worked at in the same way as the other three. Beat up the centre of rosette first with No. 5 punch, the ovate sections dependent upon it with No. 8, the laurel leaves running round the outer part with No. 12, the beads at the points of rosette and berries with No. 3, and the stem, from which the leaves shoot, with No. 10.

Fig. V., another simple arrangement for a pin-tray, is drawn to illustrate the progressive stages. The centre of rose and six petals (see one marked 'c') should be raised first—the petals slightly—with No. 5 punch;

FIG. V.

next the leaves, round outer part, along the two sides (see one marked 'a') with No. 8 tool, leaving the edges and centres; then the band round centre of rose and stems arranged round outer part of tray, and those coming from under the leaves, with No. 11. No. 12 should now be used for the ends of the petals that turn over (see one marked 'd') and parts that divide the petals and veins in centres of petals (see the form finished) with No. 10. No. 7 should be used last for the veins in leaves (see one marked 'b') and afterwards for the serrations to mark them as the four leaves finished. All the foregoing examples are intended to be worked from the back.

CHAPTER III.

CHASING AND REPOUSSÉ.

In the two foregoing chapters reference is made solely to the simplest methods of obtaining effective results by shaping the ornament with blunt punches from the back only. By itself, however, such a method can but produce indefinite forms; and if a pronounced delineation of ornament is desired, tracers and other punches

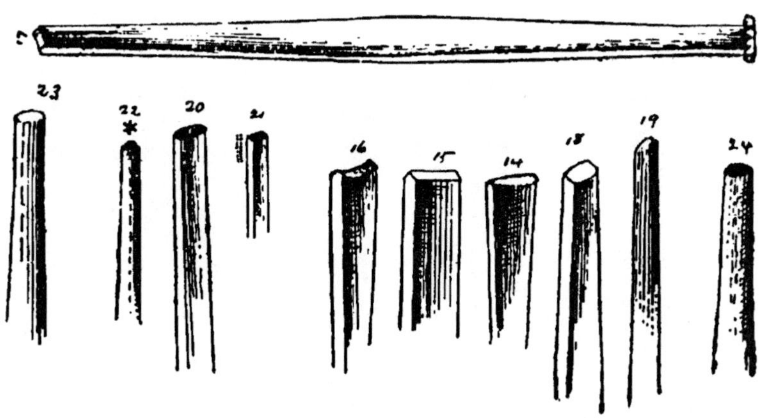

must be used (see Nos. 14 to 24); Nos. 14, 15, 16, and 18 are tracers, No. 19 a loop-punch, Nos. 20 and 21 grain mats, No. 22 a star-punch, No. 24 a mixed mat for groundwork, and No. 23 a planisher used for modelling ornament from the front and back. Fig. I. has been beaten out of a piece of zinc, 6 size, in a Birmingham metal gauge-plate for the purpose of illustrating the different stages of work ; A is left from beating the back only ; B, after being raised from the back in the same way, has been traced round the outlines with Nos. 17 and 18 punches, and modelled into shape with them and No. 23 punch ; C is left from the outline in an unfinished condition ; while D has been first outlined on the front, and raised from the back without the aid of any additional finishing on the front : E has been treated in exactly the same way, but finished afterwards from the front with tools of similar shapes to Nos. 17 and 18 to trace round the outline ; and grain and mixed mats, such as Nos. 20, 21, and 24, to produce what is known as a soft appearance.

FIG. I.

A grain mat (see Nos. 20 and 21) is a punch with the end that is used on the work covered with small rows of round or elliptical dots of even size, and arranged so that one row fits closely and regularly between the dots of the next. All punches are made of cast steel, except very large ones used for raising, and which are sometimes made of boxwood or horn; but although suited for the purpose of raising large masses, they lack the solidity that steel ones always carry with them. The steel can be obtained from any steel warehouse in rods from one foot to six feet in length, varying in thickness from one-eighth of an inch upwards, either square, hexagon, or round shaped. Although it is frequently a greater convenience and saving of time to purchase the blanks forged into their various shapes, as the ends or faces have only then to be formed. The very best blanks I have seen were supplied by a Sheffield firm named Taylor.

When the steel is bought from the warehouse, or in ready-forged blanks, it is always advisable to soften it before making it into finished punches by heating it red hot, and laying it in ashes to cool slowly. This will render it much easier to file, and make it less liable to blunt and wear the tools used upon it for shaping.

The whole of the punches used by the most skilful professional workers in repoussé are made by them, but most are glad to buy good ready-forged blanks.

A grain mat is a very delicate piece of work, and requires great skill to make it well. The end is first filed smoothly into the shape required, and matted lightly all over with a very fine mixed mat that has been formed by another mixed mat. This effaces any mark left by the file, and gives a smooth and even surface. It is then struck by a tool with a double row of projecting dots, which again is made by a punch with counter dots, viz., a sharp mat; but when it has been struck with this, the projecting dots are not very pronounced, and to make them so they are struck separately with a small ring or pippin-shaped punch, as the case may require, and the exact size of the dot. This method makes each individual dot perfect, and a watchmaker's three-square file is used last to remove the surplus metal at the sides, so that each row, looking at it from the side, presents the appearance of very minute teeth. It is now hardened by heating red hot and immersing it into soapsuds. The side is then rubbed on emery cloth near the end with the dots on for the purpose of brightening, and is held in the gas about one inch or one and a half inches from the end and watched until the brightened part becomes straw-coloured, when it should be quickly immersed again into suds, and afterwards tried close to the end with a file to be quite certain that it is hard; if it is, the file will slip over it without making any impression. This method of hardening applies to all punches. There are others, but we do not know of a better than the one described. Care, however, should be taken not to get the punch *white* hot, for in the event of so doing it will "burn" the steel and make it scaly and spoil the face.

The tool is now ready for making the mat, which is done by first striking it firmly along the middle to make an impression of the two rows of dots. The left hand row is now fitted into the row of counter ones on the right hand side of the mat, and struck again, which produces a third row, and so on until that side of the mat is covered, when it should be turned and again worked at from left to right in the same way. Each hole is then cleared by striking it very lightly with a single pick. The mat is then ready for hardening. A mixed mat or freezer is made by striking it on the end lightly by another mixed mat with blows in rapid succession until the face is evenly covered. A single pick is then struck all over indiscriminately until one hole breaks into the other.

The tracers 14, 15, 16, 17, and 18 are filed into various shapes at the ends, and afterwards whetted on an oil-stone. Of course the smoother the file used last before stoning the less whetting on the stone to give smoothness will be required. For such a one as 16, that is concaved at one side, the oilstone is rounded along one edge—Turkey stone is the best for the purpose. After whetting on the stone it should be rubbed on a piece of rouged buff-leather, usually glued on to a piece of hard wood some eight inches long by three inches wide and half an inch thick—allowing a margin of a quarter of an inch at the sides and ends of the leather. The tracers are always cleaned and brightened by "buffing": the mats by striking them on ground pumice or crushed embers mixed with oil on a cake of lead. A spot of turps is then applied by the tip of the finger, afterwards dried with a little clean rag, and rubbed with a piece of bottled-india-rubber for the purpose of cleaning it thoroughly and removing all ash collected in hardening.

Fig. II. is from a photograph of the famous Flemish salver, a work of the seventeenth century, the original is in South Kensington Museum. There is, perhaps, no more beautiful example of repoussé in existence than this. Its mastery evinces at once to the trained eye in repoussé that the executant knew and accomplished the very important position of a workman before attempting that of an artist, and thereby attaining the highest stage of the latter through the acquired knowledge of the former. An undeniable proof of this is expressed in the splendid disposition of the ornament, the skilful variation, which has not been permitted to interfere with the balancing of the design as a whole, and, perhaps, above all, the wonderful amount of feeling that is shown in the foliage and flowers with the smallest possible amount of labour. The shape of the salver, too, is very happily adapted to ornamentation, and, doubtless, was made by the same hands that decorated it.

It is 13½ inches in diameter with a well 6¾ inches wide, half an inch in depth; and it may be made by the student in the following way:—Describe a circle $13\frac{1}{2}$ inches in diameter and an inner one of $6\frac{3}{4}$ inches for the well, cut with the snips the metal away to the outer circle, beat carefully inside the well with a box-wood mallet with rounded ends, on a sandbag, viz., a

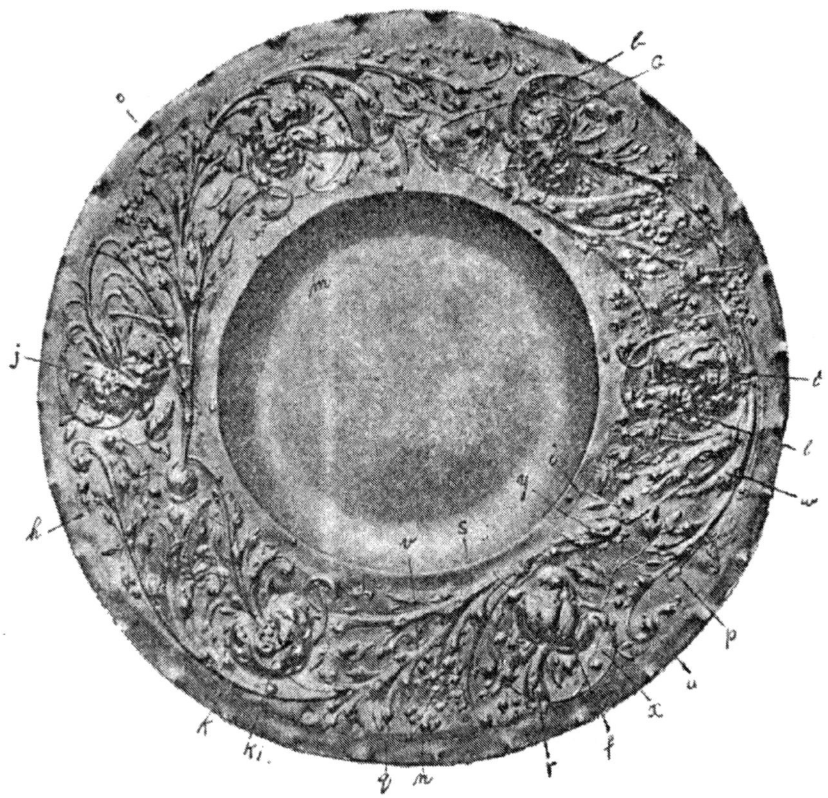

FIG. II.

round cushion made of strong leather filled with sand, and securely stitched all round the edge so as to prevent the sand from escaping (see D on Plate I., Chapter I.). When the well is thus roughly shaped it should be beaten with a planishing hammer with slightly rounded face upon a lump of modelling wax, a mixture of beeswax 1lb., white wax ½lb., resin ¼lb., pitch ¼lb., Venice turps half a teacupful, and tallow added to consistency required—the softer it is required the more fat should be added.

Although a silversmith would use steel anvils or "stakes" of suitable shapes to finish after the sandbags, and by this latter means the smoothest possible surface can be obtained. When formed it should be rubbed with emery cloth, and afterwards with a piece of pumice stone and water. And if at finishing, it is rubbed in small circles, the marking on of the design will be easier. The two lines *h* and *i* should be ruled with the compasses and it is then ready to be stuck on to the cement. The pitch on the block should be thicker than the well is deep and wider than the dish. A hole in the middle of the cement rather larger than the well and as deep should be chipped out with a sharp chisel to admit it. The pitch—which should be allowed to stand awhile after melting, so as to become rather thick—should be poured into the well and over the other part, and the dish pressed quickly into it. When the block is quite free from cement or has only one layer on it, a hole may be formed to receive the well by pouring circular layers wider than the flat part of the salver, until the cement becomes as thick as the well is deep, and the hole in the middle wide enough to receive it.

When it is ready for decorating, the two corded serpentine lines *h* and *i* should be made with a dot same shape but smaller than No. 2, Chapter I. When done, strike a line round the band at equal distance from the lines *h* and *i* to serve as a guide, and divide it into six equal parts; on these divisions draw the husks or bosses, *e*, *g*, *t*, *f*, *k*, and *j*: next the foliated scrolls that connect them, first with single lines as guides, afterwards adding the details of foliage. When the design is all drawn on, a blunt tracer, but of the shape of 14 (see commencement of the present Chapter), should be used for the long and all slightly curved lines, such as *s*, *p*, and *v*, a smaller tracer of the same shape may be found of greater advantage for such delicate parts as *x*. And the remainder of the outline can be executed with No. 17. The loopholes, such for instance as *y*, should be struck in with a punch shaped as 19, and the tracer that has been used for the long curves, run down the leaves as a principal vein, see *w*. Before releasing the dish to work from the back, the ground should be matted with a "soft" or worn mixed mat. A newly made mat may be made to give the appearance of a worn one by using it while soft upon hard metal, or rubbed upon ground pumice, or brickdust on wood. And now will be seen the great skill of the author of the Flemish salver. With the exception of the bosses *e*, *g*, *t*, *f*, *k*, and *j*, the work has been finished from the back. The long pipes, such as *s* and *w*, have been beaten up with such punches as 10 and 11 (see Chapter I.), while 2, 3, and 4, for such parts as *d*, *b*, *c*, *p*, *u*, *n*, and *q*, 8 for *r*; and first 5, 8, and 9, for the masses, in *e*, *g*, *t*, *f*, *k*, and *j*, and afterwards with such punches as 3 and 2, as will be seen distinctly in *e*, *j*, *k*, and *t*. The crimp round the edge *o*, *o*, *o*, has been produced by a tool such as 12, but crimped edges may be varied on similar shapes to an almost unlimited extent, by striking the same punch on the front instead of the back, in an oblique direction by striking from the back, tool No. 8 between *o*, (see *o*, *x*, and *o*, *x*). Of course, the last suggestions are for any work that will admit of crimping. In the parts *t* and *k* may be seen the slight working that the ornament has had from the front, and although *j*, *e*, *g*, and *f*, have also gone through a like process, the identification is extremely faint. And the exquisite freedom of form given to such parts as *q*, *p*, *u*, *d*, *w*, and *f*, with so small an amount of labour, pronounces at once the workman to be an artist in metal of the very highest order. Indeed the Flemish salver stands out alone in its style—which is beautiful in its simplicity and elegant in its beauty.

I am indebted for the loan of the work given in Fig. III. to the courtesy of Mons. Auguste Willms, chief designer at Messrs. Elkington & Company's works, Birmingham. It is an unfinished work in silver—a descending demon—by the late Morel Ladeuil. The highest

FIG. III.

part is not more than one-sixteenth of an inch above the unworked surface of the metal. It has been first outlined with such shaped tracers as 18 and 14, but smaller than 14. After outlining it has been beaten from the back in parts—restuck on the cement and a soft mixed mat used round most of the outline. The cloud on the right side of the figure has been raised round the edges of the outline by such a tracer as 17, but that cloud under the left arm has not been raised at all from the back, but beaten back from the front round the edge with a narrow mixed mat, as indicated by the broad black line. There are spots on the right wing, the knuckles, and wristbone of the right hand and arm, the joints of the left hand, the eye, nostrils, hair, and spots on the breast, toes, and tail, which have been produced with a single dot as No. 2, and left from the back. Although not very discernible in the illustration, the marks about the arms and trunk are the first indications of modelling from the front with a tool similar to a soft mixed mat. The work is most masterly in its direct treatment. And in a later chapter we shall give more elaborate specimens of Morel Ladeuil's famous works.

Fig. IV. is also from a photograph, an acanthus leaf, worked in steel out of 8 B. M. G., and its original size seventeen inches by ten. The artist is Mr. William Stace, until very recently employed by Messrs. Elkington & Co., at their premises in Newhall Street, Birmingham, as a designer, modeller, and worker in repoussé, and also employed by them now in the latter on figure subjects, at intervals off the premises; he is also master of one of the branch schools of art in Birmingham. His works in repoussé—of which we shall give several examples—are most refined in their treatment as evinced in this first illustration. We give it as one of the choicest specimens of grain-matting that has ever come under our notice. It has been outlined first with a rather blunt tracer, restuck on the cement, and then first roughly modelled by a planisher that has been allowed to rust, to give it the texture of a very much worn mixed mat, and afterwards matted with a soft-grain mat from the base of the leaf to its extremities. The pipes have been put in from the back (after partly forming them on the front), with such tools as 6, 10, and 11. The ground has been made with a similar tool to 22, and the stem from which the foliage

Fig. IV.

springs with smooth planishers; and below are illustrations from photographs of 14 punches, some of which were used on the leaf above. It is a most beautiful work, more especially when the hardness of the metal, after any hammering, is taken into consideration.

CHAPTER IV.

CHASING AND REPOUSSÉ.

FIGS. I. and II. are sections enlarged from the Flemish dish given in the last chapter, with the hope that the means by which the results have been obtained will be more clearly seen by a student. All the parts to which the letters made reference are there ex-

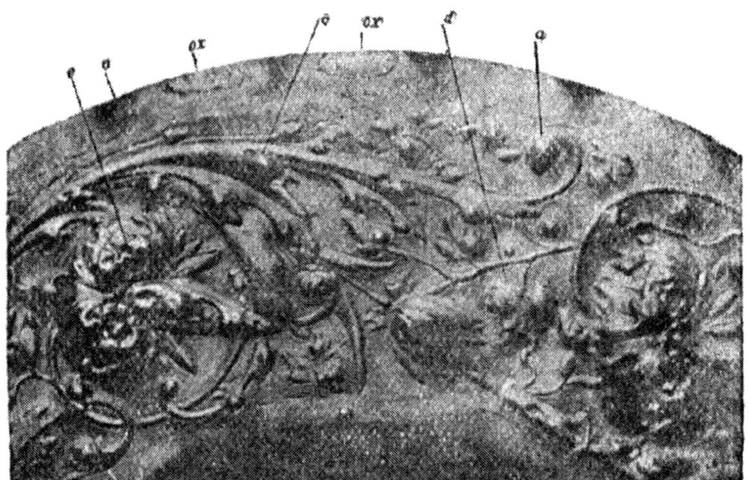

FIG. I.

plained, and to further illustrate crimping we give an oval trinket dish, $7 \times 4\frac{1}{2}$ (Fig. III.). A is the same as the crimp round the Flemish salver; B, C, and D are all obtained, like A, by striking the metal on the back.

Fig. II.

Fig. III.

The narrow divisions in B are obtained by using a straight tracer, such as No. 15, and those in D a curved one, such as No. 14 (see last chapter), and in C and the broader parts of B and D, by tools such as No. 8, but suited in size to the crimp. They may all be done on

FIG. IV.

the cement, but a cleaner way is to make counter punches to screw in a vice, and forcing the metal into them by striking the edge with tools of counter shapes. This method will require some one to hold the article in position while the worker is striking the crimps. The dish may be made, too, by the student on the same lines as described while referring to the Flemish salver; and the raising—after the dish is shaped—of the oval in the centre, first by a punch made of buckhorn or steel, while the cement is warm.

Fig. IV. is a suggested design for a pin tray, the

FIG V

ground matted with a single pick, such as No. 2. The trays may be obtained in brass, ready for decoration, at a nominal cost, from Mr. Green, Caroline Street, and several brassfounders in Birmingham.

Fig. V. is a design for a portrait frame, in which we give five different kinds of groundings. The panel at each corner has been done with a small ring tool, that portion on the right-hand side with a small straight tracer struck four times one way and four times at right angles, and again at right angles to the last struck, and

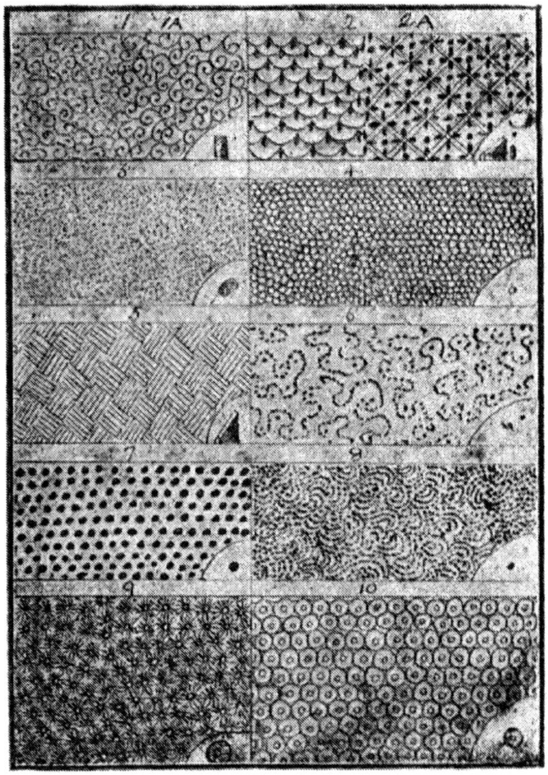

Fig. VI.

so on until the ground is entirely covered, representing a kind of basket-work or "wicker" work. The ground on the left side of the frame is obtained by matting all over, first with a mixed mat, No. 24 (see Chapter III.) and afterwards running in a serpentine way, as indicated in illustration, a pointed punch, as No. 1, Chapter I., but whetted to a pyramidical shape on the end; and, if five or six flat sides are added to the minute pyramid by an additional whetting, they will serve as facets, and give a sparkle to the dotted line when wrought upon the dead ground work produced by the mixed mat. The grounding at the top can be produced by a single pick (No. 2, Chapter I.). Start at one corner, and form the back of a scroll, or section of a circle, with a dotted line; fill in the inside with parallel lines, run another row to form an outside line, but in a different direction to the first, fill in in the same way, and so continue until the ground is covered. The grounding given at the bottom can be produced by first going over it with a fine mixed mat, and then using a small half-round shaped tracer, whetted up to a rather sharp edge, beginning at one corner, as in that at the top, and starting one scroll from another until the ground is covered.

To make the illustration of groundings more palpable I give in Fig. VI. twelve different kinds, with the ends of the punches in the corners of the ten panels.

Before concluding the remarks concerning the portrait frame, I would remind the student that a margin of metal of at least an inch should be allowed for working, and after the repoussé is finished the cleanest way of cutting it out round the outline is with a metal fret-saw.

CHAPTER V.

CHASING AND REPOUSSÉ.

FROM personal experience and information received from those who teach in technical schools, the student is very frequently at a loss for a design best suited to the material and the shapes of the articles he or she has to decorate; and therefore we feel it very essential to give original designs from time to time together with reproductions of photographs from specimens of the actual works in repoussé by the most skilful artists that we can bring within our reach. Our means, however, of reproducing some of the larger specimens of the choicest works are limited, owing to the space they would occupy; but we hope by the specimens we do give, whether in sections or as complete articles, the student's interest will be sufficiently aroused to prompt him or her to see the originals, or electro deposits of them, which will be very nearly of equal value. Fig. I is a section from a photograph of a salver of the school of Cellini, accounted by some writers to him; but many works are said to be from his hand which are surrounded with doubt, and the best proof is simply based on conjecture. It is, however, worthy to be a work of the great master, although the treatment differs in many respects from many of the productions that are known to be his. The subject of the design is Orpheus with his lyre moving birds, trees, beasts and fishes by the skilful charm of his music. The principal figure in the well of the salver is the mythological god, seated on rockwork—with beasts, waves, fishes, men, birds and trees surrounding him in a quaintly mixed fashion—but the bas-relief that forms the border of the dish gives expression to a mastery

FIG. I.

over set design. Six panels arranged with ornamental shaped outline are filled with different kinds of animals, while the spaces between are well disposed by bands terminating in dolphins' heads and scroll endings, and from them and bills of birds are suspended festoons of drapery and flowers. The whole of the work has been finished with "soft" punches from the front, as described in doing similar work in a previous chapter.

In Fig. II. we give another reproduction of a photograph from a shield—the work of Cellini—and, as he undoubtedly was as great amongst workers in metal as Shakespeare amongst poets, we may be allowed a few brief remarks concerning him.

He was born at Florence in the year 1500—sixty-four years before Shakespeare was born to us by the side of the Avon, and at the opening of the great galaxy of men of art and letters—but the morals of the time were bad, and Cellini was no exception to the evils that ruled the society of his age. According to his autobiography he was in morals and manners the extreme opposite to our Shakespeare, who won for himself the prefix of "the gentle." With Cellini it should perhaps have been "the riotous." At an early part of his life he was banished from Florence and went to Rome; he was allowed to return, and was compelled to fly to Rome a second time, where he gained the favour of Clement VII. He tells us that he killed, at the siege of Rome, the Constable Bourbon and Prince of Orange—being as great in arms as art—but his recklessness compelled his constant moving between Rome, Florence, Mantua and Naples. He went to the Court of France in 1537. He returned to Rome and was imprisoned on a charge of plundering the treasures in the Castle of St. Angelo during the siege of Rome. He was delivered by Cardinal Ferrara, with whom he went to France. After again settling matters with his sword, he returned to Florence, where he executed several beautiful works in metal and marble—notably the celebrated bronze group of "Perseus with the head of Medusa"—which now adorns the market-place in Florence. He died in 1570-72. It is strange to contemplate the reckless,

Fig. II.

passionate nature of Cellini, with the extreme patience that he must have bestowed upon his works of art. Yet had he been an unimpassioned man, the realistic feeling exhibited in his works had not been. We have this too to consider: He not only made a cup from forged gold or silver, but ornamented it with chasing, repoussé, enamels, or niello, as the design may have required, and set it with precious stones. He not only modelled his solid parts, such as the handles and figures for the top and base—but was a sculptor of the highest merit. The original of the shield given in Fig. II. is in silver,

FIG. III.

and about 2 feet 6 inches long by 2 feet 8 inches wide in the broadest part. The large medallion in the centre comprises a battle scene, while the four smaller ones at the top, bottom, and sides, are devoted to figures emblematic of war. The spaces at the top and bottom are covered by two elaborate masks; while on the largest parts above and below the centre are captives, and other figures moderately bold, with a background formed of trophies. The whole of the work, although not seen to the best advantage here, is very powerful in its modelling, and has been finished by working from the front last, and executed with "soft" or worn punches; but as we shall give more specimens of Cellini's work later on, we will now draw attention to a few original designs I have made with the hope of assisting the student in this direction.

Fig. III. is intended for a pin tray, and can readily be shaped in soft-rolled brass, copper, or silver, out of six or eight size B. M. G. Cut the metal out 4 ins. by $2\frac{3}{4}$ ins., rounding the sharp corners after with the snips and file, and on a piece of iron or hard wood, with two sides forming a right angle, and not so long as the width of the tray; beat all round the edge, first ruling a line with the dividers about 3-16ths ins. as a guide. It will then give the shape shown in illustration (Fig. III.). The edge standing up at right angles with the bottom, and forming at each corner a small spout as it were. It will be best to turn up the edges after the repoussé is done. Two kinds of groundings should be made, as indicated in illustration, to give variety. After outlining and matting, it may be finished from the back. The same design would serve for a trinket-box lid. Fig. IV. is intended for a letter rack. Four pieces of metal, twelve B.M.G., 4 inches by $2\frac{1}{4}$ inches, should be cut out, afterwards the semicircle at top, for the thumb and finger, with a pair of bent snips. The ornament may be put on after they are cut out, and treated in the same way as Fig. III., only that in

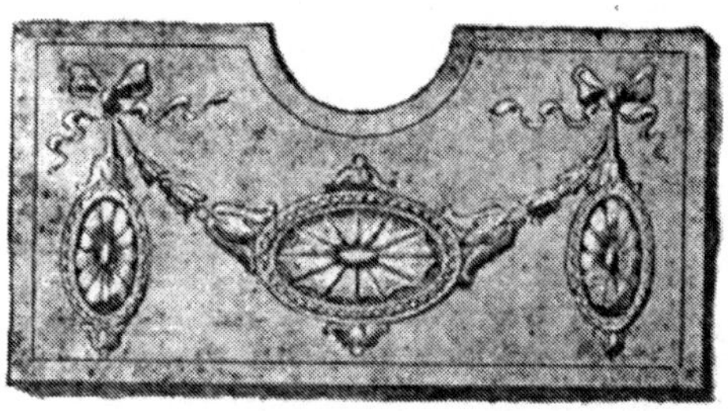

FIG. IV.

this instance the ground is intended to be left plain, not matted. A piece out of the same thickness of metal, viz., twelve B.M.G., and 8 inches or 8½ inches long, but with a semicircle projecting at top, with an inverted key-hole pieced in for the purpose of hanging up. The width, of course, should be same as the sections, as it is to form a back for them, on to which they are riveted at each bottom corner. Beginning by securing the top plate first, and bringing the top edge of the second plate slightly above the bottom of the one just fastened, and so on, until the bottom edge of the bottom plate should be flush with the large one that forms the back.

FIG. V.

Fig. V. may be made in the same way as Fig. III., the ground round the centre rosette and four small ones at the corners may be matted with one mat, and the remainder of the ground with another.

A margin should be allowed in Fig. VI., which is intended for a mirror or portrait frame. We should suggest about 14 inches by 8 inches, and ten size in a B.M.G. The straight lines should be ruled first, and the circles at corners and semicircle at bottom struck next, and then the ornament drawn at top. Punches 14, 15, 16, and 19 (see Chapter III.), should be used for outlining first, and afterwards raised from the back with numbers 5, 8, and 9 (Chapter I.). A wood back should be fastened on to secure the glass, by means of screws and nuts from the back of each rosette at the corner, and midway on sides and top and bottom.

Fig. VII. is to take the place of a tile, size 5 inches,

FIG. VI.

to fit in the side of a fire-grate, or if a small ball-foot is riveted, or soldered on to each corner, it may answer the purpose of a tea-pot stand. It can be finished

Fig. VII.

Fig. VIII.

effectively from the back, as also may the key plate, Fig. VIII.

Fig. IX. A handle plate may be finished from the back, with the exception of the mask, which should be

Fig. IX.

finished from the front, after raising from the back, and this and Fig. VIII. cut out with straight and bent snips.

CHAPTER VI.

CHASING AND REPOUSSÉ.

We are now advancing to more intricate designs, but think it wise to intersperse them with simpler ones, such, for instance, as Figs. I., II., III., and VI.; Figs. IV. and V. will be found more difficult to execute, on account of the mask and large shield on IV., and the head in the medallion in Fig. V., with the small flowers in the panel above the head, and the fruit in the one below it. While Figs. I., II., III., and VI. could be outlined, veined, and matted—on the front, of course—and finished with good effect by last beating from the back, the working on the front side always leaving the impression of the ornament sufficiently distinct on the opposite side to enable the worker to see portions that are required to be raised—excepting when the metal is unusually thick.

Fig. IV. is intended for a book-cover. The groundwork in the panels at the four corners, those at the sides of the shield, and the one at the top over the shield, should be matted with a different tool to the other part, for the purpose of contrast. It may be worked in the same way as Fig. IX. in Chapter V. Sticking on after raising from the back, to finish the mask, and planish the shield, if uneven, from the front.

Fig. I., another mirror or portrait-frame, may be treated in exactly the same way as Fig. VI. in Chapter V.

Figs. II., III., and V. are designs for finger-plates. Fig. V. should be cut out of brass or copper, twelve

Fig. I.

B.M.G., in an oblong form, as Figs. II. and III., but allowing a margin of $\frac{3}{16}$ths or $\frac{1}{4}$-inch on the outside

Fig. II.

Fig. III.

ornament, and the straight lines at the sides and ends that inclose the beads in the border ruled from the

FIG. IV.

edges of the straight lines with the spring-compasses. The two arcs at ends and sides should be struck also with the spring-compasses. This portion, together with the beads, should be done on a flat-iron or steel before sticking on the cement, because of the work coming so near the edges of the metal. If the beads were struck when on the cement, it would at once spring from it. The space between the border and ornament in centre of plate should be left plain, and the ground matting, and at the sides of the head in circle, and in the panels above and below it containing fruit and flowers, and the ornaments at top and bottom may be varied for the purpose of contrast, *e.g.*, in the circle with a dot after matting with a fine matting punch, see "7" in the specimens of grounding (Fig. VI., Chapter V.), in the panels containing fruit and flowers, with "3," and the smaller panels adjoining at top and bottom with "4." The whole plate should be sawn out with a metal fret-saw after the repoussé is finished; the head in the circle should be finished from the front. The straight lines in Figs. III. and II. should be traced in the same way as Fig. V. on iron or steel, but the plate

FIG. V.

cut out exact size before commencing the lines, as no margin is required. One ground tool should be used on Fig. III., and two on Fig. II.

Fig. VI.

Fig. VI. is an arrangement of convolvuluses for a brass or copper tray, the size of which may be determined by the student. It may either be 6, 8, 10, or 12 inches, but should be either flat chased or only very slightly raised—the ground beaten down from the front—on account of the use to which it is intended to be put. If the surface is made uneven by raising, to any high degree from the back, articles placed upon it, especially wine glasses or tumblers, would not stand well, but would be likely to slip about and fall; but by outlining with a blunt, or better, obtusely whetted tracer (see 17,

FIG. VII.

beginning of Chapter III.), and by beating the ground down evenly with a soft mixed mat, the ornament will stand out in low relief and have a very pleasing effect, especially if the flowers and leaves are modelled into form by worn grain mats, or planishers. The shading in the illustration is intended to help the student to accomplish his or her end in this respect.

If, however, the student prefers raising it from the back, the tray should be filled with cement as explained in Chapter II.

FIG. VIII.

Figs. VII. and VIII. are two more specimens by Mr. William Stace. Fig. VII. is an unfinished plaque in sheet steel, seven B.M.G. It is 6 by 7 inches, and is an allegorical treatment of Night—the queen being borne on a crescent-shaped drapery by four satellites—and is given here with the hope of imparting to the student a conception of the condition of work in its progress to a finished state. It has been first outlined with a blunt tracer, such as 17, Chapter III., and beaten up from the back, and afterwards modelled into shape by some of the tools given in Chapter VII. and "23" in Chapter III. on the front. Fig. VIII. is a finished work in sheet silver, six B.M.G., and 6 inches in diameter. It is symbolic of Morn. The idea is most poetically conceived, as in Fig. VII., and the workmanship delicate and refined.

CHAPTER VII.

CHASING AND REPOUSSÉ.

In every art there is an individuality which distinguishes one worker's productions from another's. In painting, sculpture, engraving, designing, architecture, and in chasing and repoussé, there is a distinct style in each artist's work—unless he or she is content to remain (as all start) a copyist. And no artist is more distinctly pronounced in his particular manner of treatment than the masters whom we have endeavoured to represent from time to time in these pages. Cellini, whom all workers in metal must bow to, shows a completeness and perfectness in design and its adaptability that perhaps no other goldsmith has ever shown. He had not only the exquisite cunning of the workman, but was blest with the vivid imagination of the artist, without which last mentioned gift all work must be mechanical and inanimate. And although the works in repoussé by Vechte are doubtlessly equal to any—that I have seen—executed by Cellini, Vechte confined himself to chasing and repoussé, whereas the great Italian excelled alike in all branches of decoration applied to, or made from, metals—being equally successful in nielloing, enamelling, or damascening, as in repoussé and sculpture. His shapes of cups, jugs, caskets, and, in fact, nearly all articles he designed, are of the most beautiful. And the happy fitness and disposition of his ornament adds beauty unto beauty, rendering each work most pleasing in its purity and completeness of style.

Fig. XIX.

In Fig XIX. we give a section of a silver table which was presented by the town of Birmingham as a marriage gift to Her Royal Highness the Princess of Wales. It is another specimen from the works of the great Frenchman, Morel Ladeuil, and is very characteristic of the great artist's style. His treatment of the hair and drapery will be recognizable in most of his other works by this one. The hair flows in crisp fantastic clusters of curls over each other in great profusion; and his drapery hangs on his figures in the most delicate folds, never destroying or concealing the beauty of modelling in them. It was a matter of some two years' labour, and is very highly finished from the front. The dancing figure (Fig. XX.) is fixed in the centre of the table, and, perhaps, is the cleverest part of all, being raised out of sheet metal in halves and soldered together. It was modelled first in wax, and a casting in brass obtained from the model; this was afterwards sawn into sections that could be fitted closely together again in each other so that the perfect figure might be retained and taken to pieces when required. The sheet silver was then beaten over it into a rude form, the brass force (as it is technically termed) extracted in sections, and the figure, after

FIG. XX.

the parts being soldered together, filled with cement or wax and modelled into finished shape with small repoussé punches. Of course some small aperture would be left in the figure to admit the cement or wax—I believe the arms were worked separately from the

FIG. XXI.

body and soldered on at the shoulders—in the event of which the cement could be poured in at the parts where the arms were joined on, and the seams made by the joining readily repaired—being but slight marks—when the figure was quite hollow, the cement having been emptied from it to allow the soldering.

Fig. XXI. is the centre of the famous Milton shield. It is in very high relief and greatly undercut in parts, and was first beaten over a brass model in the same way as the dancing figure referred to above, the draping of the angel is very beautifully rendered; but Morel's modelling loses in delicacy and life-like vibration in this,

Fig. XXII.

as in many other of his works, when compared with the exquisite productions of his master, Mons. Vechte, who is the author of the adjoining specimen (Fig. XXII.). It is a portion of the national medallion used as an award for success in the National Art Competition. Nothing finer has ever been produced, to our knowledge, than this, and the distinction between the modelling in it and in Morel's (Figs. XIX. and XXI.) will easily be recognized. The muscular force exhibited in the figures in action, as may be seen in the one at the top

FIG. XXIII.

of this specimen, cannot be too highly praised—his figures breathe as it were in tremulous emotion.

Turning now for a moment from illustrations of actual works, we give a few original designs adapted for the decoration of articles of use. Fig. XXIII., a

Fig. XXIV.

Fig. XXV.

Fig. XXVI.

Fig. XXVII.

design for a military hairbrush-back, may be finished from the back with good effect; but as the work is rather small, and the article one that must be constantly under close observation, a better result will be gained by planishing the scrolls forming the centre ornament to an angle with a flat planisher, and the remaining scrolls and leaves may be modelled to advantage into more delicate forms by punches such as No. 36, page 63. Figs. XXV., XXVI., and XXVII. may be treated at the discretion of the student, either by finishing from the back or front, as referred to in foregoing chapters. Fig. XXIV. is intended for the front plate of a pair of bellows, to be executed in 7 or 8-sized metal in a B.M.G. plate. This should be worked on the front last on account of the mask; but a margin of at least an inch should be allowed all round the shape to admit of working, which should afterwards be cut off to the outline with the snips. Fig. XXV., a finger plate in 11 or 12 gauge. Figs. XXVI. and XXVII. are lock and finger plates, and should be made in metal of the same thickness, or on account of their size a little thicker may be used with advantage to give greater strength. The semi-rosettes at the top and bottom corners and the outside corners of the part of the plate that covers the lock in Fig. XXVI. may have the ground between them and the bands sawn away with a fret saw or cut through with a small sharp chisel whetted straight on one side and slightly curved on the other (see Chapter X.). The work of piercing should be performed after the repoussé is finished in most instances. If sawn or chiselled through before the ornament is raised it will break where tied or connected frequently in raising. The ornament at the top and bottom and right angles formed by the plate for the lock and the finger parts in XXVII. should be sawn, not chiselled, owing to the ornament being so much more slender in its connections or ties than in XXVI., and therefore much more liable to break in chiselling than sawing; for it will be seen in the former method in making the first incision with the chisel the metal it displaces must be forced on one side

FIG. XXVIII.

or the other to make way for it; whereas in the latter a small hole is drilled between each tie and the surplus metal sawn away, leaving undisturbed the ornamented parts, which the use of the saw has made much more emphatic; but to saw out the greater portion of a design for a finger plate cannot be recommended, as the edges are liable to catch the fingers and the recesses to hold the dirt that cannot be readily removed, although plates with a large amount of sawing in the designs have been somewhat fashionable, and we give an original one in Chapter X. by Mr. J. R. Duffield.

Fig. XXVIII. is from a photograph of a cupid executed in zinc, 6 size B. M. G., by Mr. William Stace, and is the property of Mons. A. Willms. It was originally intended to form a medallion in a design for a finger plate executed in brass or copper, and the student may readily conceive the charming contrast of such metals—the richness of the copper, or even brass, against the subdued soft grey of the zinc—although it has not been completed. Many goods are now manufactured combining iron and copper, and copper and brass, with very effective results, and where the worker is not bound by commercial limits, the most successful artistic ends may be acquired by discreet contrast of various metals such as has never yet been attempted. The face of the cupid stands well out from the ground in clean relief, being most cleverly undercut, the right hand is engaged in drawing an arrow from the quiver, while the left is occupied in holding the bow. Fifteen tools are here given from photographs of actual punches, some of which have been

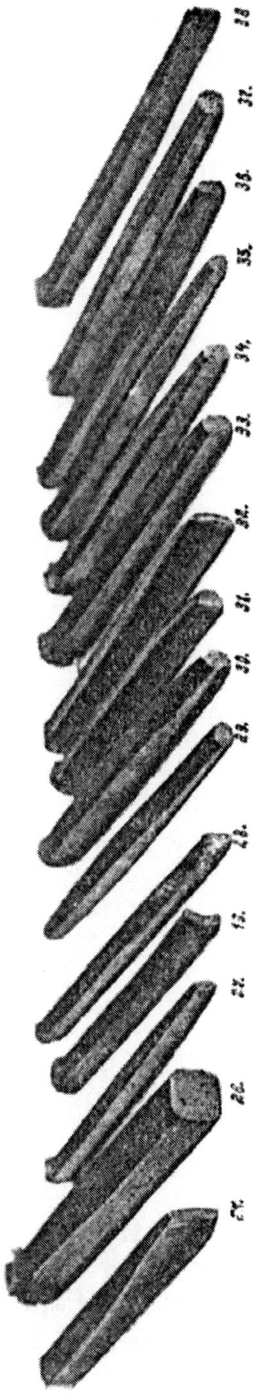

used on the works by Mr. Stace illustrated in this volume.

Fig. XXIX. is from a plaque, 6 inches in diameter, by a Mr. Waite, and is one of the most wonderful performances that has yet come under our notice; for the

FIG. XXIX.

reason that the artist was purely an amateur, being by profession a civil engineer. It is intended for a portrait in profile of the great engineer, Robert Stephenson, and was executed in copper, about 10 gauge, on a sandbag and wax. The weakest part is the hair, which is a little hard and wooden, but on the whole it is a most clever performance, and should prove a strong incentive to all students who take up this fascinating art as an accomplishment, apart from their every-day vocation.

CHAPTER VIII.

CHASING AND REPOUSSÉ.

THE Amazon Dish given below in Fig. XXX., and an enlarged section in Fig. XXXI., has justly gained a fame equal to that of any modern or perhaps ancient produc-

FIG. XXX.

tion ever executed in repoussé. It is the work of the celebrated Frenchman, Antoine Vechte, as is also Fig.

FIG. XXXI.

XXXII. The Amazon Dish (as stated in the Introduction) was designed by his fellow-countryman,

Jean Feuchere, who was an accomplished statuary, designer, and decorator. And the plaque (Fig. XXXII.) is an arrangement of figures chosen from the drawings by Flaxman. For although Vechte was so marvellously skilful as a worker in repoussé, and indeed we owe to his genius the revival of

FIG. XXXII.

this splendid art, he was not accounted either a designer or draughtsman. Yet his modelling is second to none, and his performances in repoussé will compare favourably with any modern or even ancient work ever produced—*not* excepting those of the great Cellini.

The great delicacy and refinement of his treatment is deserving of the highest praise, and his vigour is unsurpassed. There is a fulness of developed strength, as it were, in his performances, that Morel Ladeuil, although he worked for Vechte, and tried to imitate him in many respects, never acquired. And in the Amazon Dish this power is most notably portrayed. The severe angular muscles of the male combatants are given in exquisite contrast with those softer rounded limbs of the female warriors, and the bound captive, forming the centre of the dish, has features of a most pitiable expression symbolic of vanquished. Our regret is that the restriction to space will not allow a full-size illustration to do this great artist greater justice, but as I have remarked in another chapter of this volume, I hope the student will try and see, where possible, for herself or himself, the originals of the works given, or electro deposits.

Fig. XXXIII. is from a salver in zinc, 6 inches in diameter, the property of Mons. A. Willms. It is the performance of another Frenchman, one Mainfroy, who is spoken of by those who knew him personally, and saw him at his work, as being one of the most direct workers in repoussé. He plainly conceived what he was about to do before commencing his subject, and went without hesitation from the beginning to the end in most instances. He was employed by Messrs. Elkington until his death, which took place some twenty years ago.

The rim of the dish is embellished with rose-leaves and roses, and is cleverly undercut in parts which gives it the appearance of being modelled and laid on to the flat surface instead of being beaten, as it is, out of the thin sheet zinc, which is about 8-metal gauge. An ornamental letter "G" with a crown above it is worked in the centre, and round the outer part of the well is a conventional arrangement of leaves forming a border, and it will be noted that the decoration of this portion is kept in low relief, with the object of not detracting from the importance the arrangement of roses is intended to hold. Figs. XXXIV., XXXV. and XXXVI. are also from works by the same artist. Fig. XXXIV. is a watch-stand

Fig. XXXIII.

decorated by an arrangement of foliated scrolls and coat-of-arms at the top and mask at bottom. Fig. XXXV., a maiden engaged in a performance of the "egg dance." It is executed in silver, apparently intended for a panel to be fixed in some work not completed. It is in keeping with Mainfroy's best works, beautifully simple in its directness. The figure is draped in silken gauze, which hangs from the short waist in fine natural folds to below the knees, and forms a graceful festoon on either side by being looped up by the hands. Four eggs are placed at the dancer's feet, and a laurel wreath in low relief is worked on

FIG. XXXIV.

either side. Fig. XXXVI. is a medallion 3 inches in diameter, and like the former work, I should say, intended to be fixed in some contemplated work in metal. Fig. XXXVII. is a pin-dish, the decoration comprising a hen and brood and a laurel border. It is not, however, so happy in its execution as the other examples.

I am indebted to Mons. A. Willms for the specimens given of his works in this volume.

Fig. XXXVIII. is a combination of repoussé and etching by Mr. F. G. Jackson, author of "Lessons on Design," Second Master at the Birmingham Municipal School of Art, and to whose kindness I owe the

FIG. XXXV.

representation of this example. The Druid's head in the centre is in repoussé, and is executed with exquisite feeling and care, and consequently is in keeping with all other works by this wonderfully clever artist. The other ornament on the plaque is etched and is purely Celtic in style. We shall have occasion in

Fig. XXXVI.

Fig. XXXVII.

another volume to refer to Mr. Jackson when dealing with etching and other methods of decoration.

Fig. XXXIX. is an original design for a fireplace panel, by Mr. J. R. Duffield, an old pupil of Mr. Jackson, and at present Assistant Master in the Sheffield School of Art. It will be observed that the design throughout is symbolic of the purpose for which it is intended, and "grows" out of the ornamental grate at the base — the medallion with the cupid blowing with the bellows is borne on a pedestal arising out of the flames. Continuing upwards is a happily designed vase containing fire from which a phœnix is rising, and on either side of the base is posed a fire dragon, and a long torch springs from each side of the grate at bottom. It may be made by the student out of any of the sheet metals mentioned, and in the size determined by the space beside the fire it is intended to fill. I should recommend the thickness of metal to 10 or 12 M.G. Fig. XL. is a simple arrangement for the top of a trinket box, and the ornament on the narrow strip is for the ends and sides.

The beautiful plaque (Fig. XLI.) is by Morel Ladeuil, and I owe its presence here to the kindness of Messrs. Elkington and Company. It is, in my mind, the most charming of all Morel Ladeuil's numerous works. It is in repoussé silver and damascened steel. The design is well conceived and the rendering softly delicate to a marked degree. And although executed in metals it seems to be enveloped in a balmy atmosphere, and bears a charm of poetry over the senses of the observer such as is experienced when viewing beautiful works in painting. The artist has illustrated in the form of a metal plaque, Pompeian life and manners. The luxurious ease of a Pompeian court devoted to the fairer portion of the household are depicted here. The Nubian slaves, the lady's handmaidens in attendance upon their fair mistress, are

Fig. XXXIX.

Fig. XXXVIII.

Fig. XL.

readily distinguished by the type of feature, most cunningly portrayed by Morel. One is placing a golden circlet upon her brow, another fastening on her sandals, while a third is holding the virgin's robe. The lady has already a bead necklace in the form of the Greek Amphoræ, round her neck, and in her hand

FIG. XLI.

she holds a polished metal mirror and apparently is delighted with her reflected beauty and the progress her maidens are making in the adornment of her form. The time chosen by the artist is evidently after the morning bath, made famous in Pompeian history. The group of figures stand out in bold relief, and the perspective of the Corinthian columns are really very wonderful. On the right side of the apartment is a tripod bearing a vase filled with choice exotics, while on the left side is splendidly rendered in low relief a statue representing the celebrated Dancing Faun. And from the capitals of the marble pillars festoons of flowers hang gracefully and luxuriantly from capital to capital, ending by turning round the front column at the left of the plaque. The whole of this scene is in silver repoussé highly finished, with soft tools on the front. The rim, or outer part of the plaque, is in damascened steel. The price of the original, which is in the possession of Messrs. Elkington and Company, is 1500*l.* For enlarged engraving of centre see Frontispiece.

CHAPTER IX.

SNARLING.

All works dealt with in these chapters until now have been flat, or of such shapes that have enabled the worker to raise the ornament upon them with a hammer and punch, struck direct on to those parts of the metal desired to be in high relief. Such means, however, are not applicable to such shapes as the following.

Fig. I. is given as a first design for snarling. The student may either raise it after tracing out and finishing from the front, or may draw the ornament on with a "scriber" (see punch No. 1, Chapter I.), and snarl up the parts before filling the vase with cement. By adopting the latter method the forms may be modelled into much more delicate shapes with the small punches.

The snarling iron should be screwed tightly in a vice at the point C, and struck sharply at point B, with the hammer held in the right hand, and that part of the ornament the student wishes to raise pressed firmly against it at point A. This implement (see Fig. A, p. 80), although called "iron," is invariably made of steel, iron soon breaks, not being capable of resisting the strain put upon it; and the snarls should vary in size at the hooked ends and in the lengths according to the work intended to be raised *e.g.*, an iron that would be long enough to raise Figs. I., II., III., and VI. would not reach the extremities in IV. and VII.

The hook, too, on the snarling-iron should be deeper for Fig. IV., as the neck is narrow and the body wide, the long part of the iron would touch the bottom part

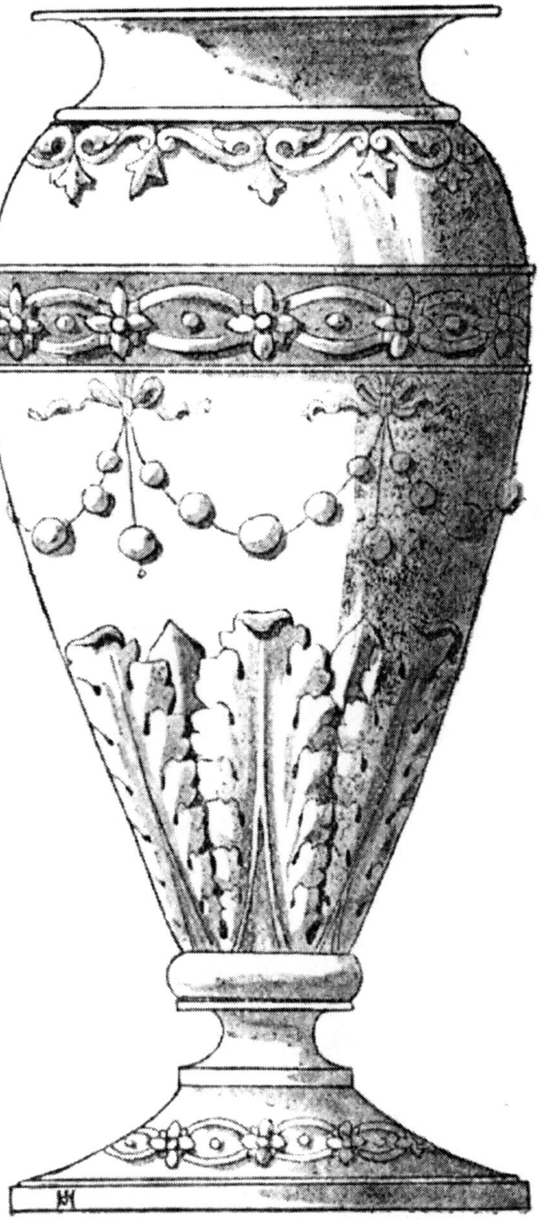

FIG. I.

of the neck and disfigure it, and the hook would not touch the part desired to be raised at the bottom of body; but in Fig. VII. the neck is so much wider than that of the jug, that the hooked end need not be bent up so far. Returning to Fig I., it will be advisable in the first attempt to raise only the rosettes in the band round the upper part of the vase, the graduated beads that form the "swags" or festoons, and the acanthus leaves at bottom.

The student should place the hooked end or nose of the snarling-iron as nearly as he can judge against the part to be raised, and strike the iron at point B Fig. A. very faintly until the exact position is ascertained, when

FIG. A.—Snarling Iron.

harder blows may be struck in accordance with the height the ornament is required. It will be found very difficult at first to gauge the exact position, but a little practice will overcome this and enable the worker to strike the position with no more trouble than he or she has in working with the other tools; but before trying on any article of value, I should recommend the student to draw some scrolls and flowers or simple arrangement of ornament upon a tin canister of some kind—a coffee or tomato tin would do very well for the purpose. When the article is very large—or of hard metal and difficult to raise—the left breast is usually pressed against it to help in guiding and steadying it, and in many instances of this description the person who has the snarling to do will obtain the services of another worker to hammer, so that both his hands may be used in holding the article during the process. This is when the iron is screwed into a vice—which is a very general way of holding it while working; but one very clever workman, named Register, a native of Sheffield, and who is now employed by the Gorham Company of Providence, U.S.A., had his "snarls" forged to sharp points at the ends, which are usually screwed into the vice, and drove them into a solid block of wood—a piece sawn off the trunk of an elm tree—similar to the blocks that are used for blacksmiths' anvils. It was customary for him to sit down to the snarling and hold the article between his knees, guiding it with the assistance of his left hand and hammering, of course, with his right. This manner of raising, however, is not a universal one, owing perhaps to the trouble of obtaining a suitable block of wood, and the room the block occupies.

Fig. II. is also a simple arrangement of the tobacco plant on a tobacco vase; the leaves and blossoms only should be raised, and finished either from the back or front. The ground work in the panels may be matted with the star punch.

Fig. III. is from a photograph of a cup, the ornament designed and executed by myself at the age of twenty. It was raised in high relief before it was outlined, and modelled into form from the front. It is executed in German silver, and, although works in such metal are now disqualified and excluded from exhibitions of art works in metal, it is one of the most difficult to work, being very hard and brittle. I am sensible of the design being weak in parts; but it was then my aim to show to those to whom I applied for work as great a variety of flowers, fruit, and ornament as I possibly could on one small article, with the object of securing employment in each or every section.

The beautiful jug, Fig. IV., page 84, by Cellini, has been, we should say, raised first before outlining, and is carefully finished from the front. The design is of the

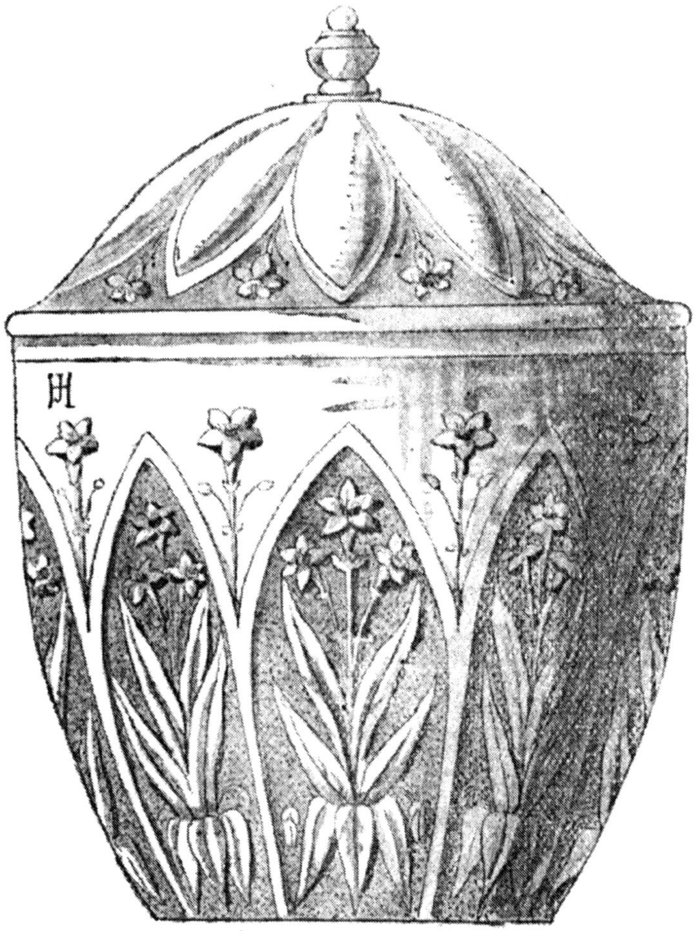

Fig. II.

highest excellence, being most graceful in form, and the decoration splendidly fitted to the shape.

Fig. V. is an illustration of a casket by the same artist with six oval panels at the sides and ends in repoussé. They may have been inserted in separate

FIG. III.

pieces from the other parts, or snarled in the same way as the former figures—but my means supplied are not sufficient to warrant a statement beyond doubt. The

Fig. IV.

design is, however, of the choicest kind, being feeble in no part and elegant as a whole.

Fig. VI. is a censer, German, of the sixteenth century, the masks, fruit, and acanthus foliage at the base have been snarled first, and finished with exquisite feeling on the front. The narrow panels between the ornaments, and round the shallow neck have been

FIG. V.

perforated with sharp chisels. It is robust in style, and characteristic of the solid German feeling.

Fig. VII. is a very recent production. It is executed in silver from a design by Mr. J. R. Duffield, who also modelled the cast parts, viz., figure of fisherman on top

Fig. VI.

and the handles. The whole of the repoussé ornament

* FIG. VII.

was executed by Mr. Ed. Bevan, of Birmingham, excepting the bas-relief of fishing scene, which was by

* A larger illustration of this cup appears on page 129.

myself. The name of the cup on neck was etched by Mr. Frank Bullivant, also of Birmingham, and the manufacture of the cup was intrusted to my care. The fishing scene was a matter of ten hours' labour, and although the ornament was of necessity hurried, it cannot bring harsh reproach, I hope, upon anyone concerned in the production, when the price, including plinth and shade was limited to 50*l*. But although the amount is very low for a cup that is 34 inches high and 14½ across its broadest part, an attempt has been made, as will be recognized, I hope, to introduce something

FIG. VIII.

apart from what is usually given for challenge cups; and I believe, Mr. Duffield, in his artistic design with the aid of conscientious workmen, has accomplished the deed.

Fig. VIII. is for a salt-cellar with three flat sides, sloping inwards, which may be slightly raised by snarling.

Fig. IX. is a section of an unfinished punch-bowl in copper by Mr. Edward Bevan. The acanthus leaf to the left is finished, and is one of the crispest representations of the acanthus in repoussé I have ever seen;

the pipes are clearly and firmly rendered, and the tips of the leaves lifted and thrown back in the most delicate manner. The leaves to the right are unfinished, and the section is given here to show to the student

FIG. IX.

the different stages of repoussé during its progress to completion. I hope Mr. Bevan will some day find an opportunity of continuing the work, and carrying to completion that which he has so beautifully begun.

CHAPTER X.

SAW-PIERCING.

THE perforating of metals by means of a fret-saw is invariably connected with chasing, repoussé, or engraving, although the three branches are seldom practised professionally by one person. In London, Sheffield, and Birmingham we find workmen calling themselves "Engravers and Saw-piercers," but it is more the exception than the rule. At one time in Birmingham the art of saw-piercing was monopolized by the male members of one family, some of whom still hold a reputation there in this profession; but young ladies are now frequently engaged by manufacturers, and with their more delicate fingers follow the calling with marked success. The saws used for the purpose can be purchased from 1*d.* to 4*d.* per dozen, but these are of foreign production, and readily break at any slight obstruction in working, so that many professionals make their own saws from watch springs with a half-round file, having the teeth on the back or rounded side ground off, and afterwards rubbed on an oil-stone to make the surface quite smooth so as to prevent the file from cutting in both directions. The saws are usually five inches long, and the thirty-second of an inch from the back to the points of the teeth (see *s*), and are secured in a bow or frame by means of a small loose plate and nuts and screws (see *r r*). A little oil should be applied to the saw to facilitate the cutting, kept at the right hand side of the worker in a shallow vessel, the lid of a small tin can is as good as anything. Bows are of various sizes, to suit the work they are required to be used on, from two and a half inches to ten and twelve inches in the direction from *p* to *s*, but the sizes most used are seven inches or eight inches and four inches (*q* to *s*). Some bows are made for special work where a constant turning or changing of

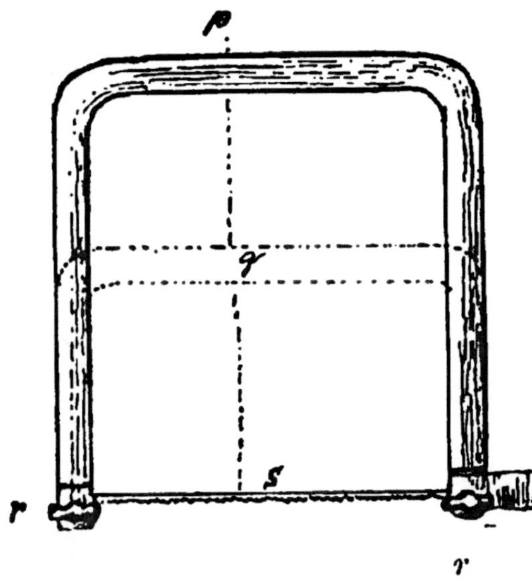

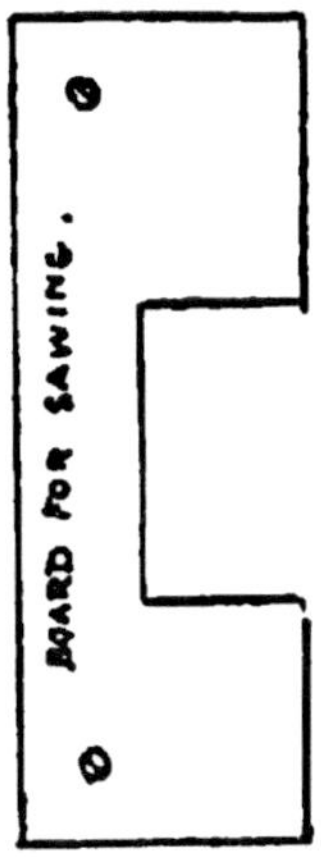

the position of the bow is required, with swivels at *r r*. The first kind of bow can be purchased for 1*s*. 6*d*., but it is a foreign production, and, like the saws, it is not of long duration; the professional, therefore, has his bows "home-made" to order.

m

With the exceptions of the fern leaf, *b*, the shamrock arrangement, *l*, and the letters M, I, Z, and H in the Mizpahs, the ornament is confined by an outer band, and in the letters P and A in the Mizpahs the small spaces at the tops of those two letters are enclosed by the outlines of the letters, as the small spaces are in *l*. On account of the minuteness of these spaces, and in *a*, *b*, the smallest ones in *g*, *h*, *i*, *j*, *k*, and Fig. IV., a small drill would be necessary to make the first perforation to admit the saw. The remainder could be made by a small punch, fixed in a press, at one blow. The Figs. II. and III. (page 94), are articles that could better be perforated with the chaser's chisel and hammer than the saw-piercer's saw, owing to their shapes. A chisel with the end shaped as *o* near Fig. II. is best suited for piercing that and Fig.

b

l

n

III. Although the perforations near the top may be sawn with success, the saw would have to be directed downward, and the task would be considered a difficult one. Pepper and sugar-castor tops can be sawn by directing the saw downwards, but these are not of any great length, and admit an amount of "play" to the saw and bow, which articles such as Figs. II. and III. will not admit. Figs. I., II., III., and IV., are from original drawings, and the remainder, except *n*, are from original works by Mr. Duern, saw-piercer, Birmingham, to whom I am indebted for the specimens given.

a

b

i

j

g

h

k

FIG. IV.

SILVER TABLE BELL

FIG II

i

FIG. III.

Fig. I. is a finger plate, by Mr. Jno. R. Duffield, now Assistant Master in the Sheffield School of Art. It is an arrangement of the lily for repoussé and saw-piercing, the blackened parts to be sawn. The ornament should be worked in repoussé first, as described in previous chapters, and when finished, sawn. After the holes to admit the saw are punched or drilled, the plate should be placed either on an oblong ¾-inch-thick board, with an incision made to allow the saw to pass freely between the two sides of the incised part (see illustration of board); or it may be held on a square-shaped peg projecting from the work-bench in the manner of a silversmith or jeweller's; or secured first in a hand-vice screwed into an ordinary vice fixed to the bench. The necessity of the hand-vice is to gain a horizontal position for the work, and to afford the worker a clear sight of what he or she is doing. Each of these methods is considered equal to the other, as they are all adopted by different workers; but I think the "peg" would be preferable for such small work as *a*, *c*, *g*, *h*, *i*, *j*, *k*, and *l*. There is a firmness, however, in the hand-vice that the other methods do not afford, and the "Mizpah" letters are sawn by Mr. Duern in this way out of a strip of gold, which is as broad as the letters are high, and long enough to cut three or

FIG I

four of the words they are intended to form. The pattern letters are sawn first out of an inexpensive metal, such as brass, and soldered in position on to another strip in two or three sets of different kinds or sizes of letters (see *m*, page 91). The tip of the finger is then rubbed on printer's ink, and patted upon the surface of the letters until they are well covered with the ink. A slip of tissue paper is then laid over them, and pressed

c

down with the finger after it has been cleansed from the ink; when the paper is removed, by taking hold at one end, the impression of the letters is secured, reading backwards as in the impression *m*, which has been taken, it will be observed, from three different sets of Mizpahs. The impression is now laid upon the strip of gold, with the inked part next the metal, exactly as it was taken from the pattern, and rubbed again gently with the finger, and carefully removed, leaving the letters printed on the gold, reading the right way. This is, to me, the best means of transferring, but some smoke the pattern over a candle or small jet of gaslight, and get an impression on tissue paper, which is gummed on the work to be sawn, and the paper pattern is pierced through. The monograms, *g, h, i, j,* which were first drawn on tracing-paper, have been gummed on to the metal, and sawn through the paper in this manner. The cross was for a pendant, the fern for a brooch, *c* for a locket back, *d* and *e* for the fronts of bracelets, *f* for a fish-carver, *k* and *l* for the principal ornaments of brooch-fronts. And the monograms may have been used for various purposes—ebony or ivory hair-brush backs, brooches or pendants. *k*, it will be observed, is reversed, showing the impression of ornament and letters as leaving the pattern; and *n* is a finger-ring, showing the letters soldered on in position and ready for the wearer. All the impressions taken from the work, it will be noticed, have the ornament represented in black, while the original drawings are the reverse of this—the portions sawn away, or chiselled, are black, as they would really appear on the articles, not in the rubbings or impressions taken in ink of them. The table-bell (Fig. IV.) could readily be sawn, indeed, such are sawn: the perforations, apart from the ornament, are supposed to emit the sound of the bell more freely. An arrangement of an iron or bell-metal fitting under the top of the silver shell, is set into motion by twisting the button on the top, and

f

H

gives a sound similar to that of an electric bell. The small black dots at the top and side of the portrait frame (Fig. V.) are the size of the punch or drill holes.

FIG. V.

Figs. II. and III. are intended for flower vases, but would, of course, require a glass fitting for each to contain the water.

CHAPTER XI.

FLAT CHASING.

Flat chasing is a name given to that kind of applied ornament, which is obtained by the use of small punches similar to those used for repoussé, as stated in Chapter I; but the tracers should be sharper on the ends, because the first outline is usually left unaltered, as corrections cannot be made with any success—

that is to say in another direction to take the place of the first—but a pleasant and artistic relief may be given to the ornament by varying the thickness of outline with tracer by hammering heavier at parts and graduating the force of blows, producing a similar effect to that given below in Fig. A, as shown at "a," "a," "a," a, and in Fig. B, "a," "a." Besides the effect gained in the skill of outlining, the varying of mats gives a great difference of colour to the metal. A slight indication of this is attempted in the flower "c" in Fig. B. Flat chasing on waiters, tea and coffee services, cups and many other articles in silver and electro plated wares was very fashionable some 30 years ago; and some professionals confined themselves entirely to this branch of decoration, and very beautiful work was produced: set designs, an arrangement of pansies, wild roses or convolvuluses, sprays or groups of flowers, upon trays, and principally set designs upon cups, claret jugs and such like vessels. And by the contrast of grain mats—streaky mats, dead mats, or mixed mats—and a varying of the strength of outline a richness was obtained, which is not in the province of engraving to produce. But an abundance of cheap and trashy work was called for and produced, which, no doubt, did much to injure flat chasing of a superior kind; for chasing to most people in the commercial world is chasing, "As hounds, and greyhounds, mongrels, spaniels, curs, shoughs, water-rugs and demi-wolves are classed all by the name of dogs," as Macbeth hath it. I have myself seen, and even executed, when a boy, brass waiters 12in. in diameter for sixpence each, and the waiters in question were literally covered with ornament. The quality of the work may be surmised by the quantity. Let us hope then, if the disgust felt for cheap and inartistic work has brought with its downfall, that of a better kind, the love for it is not dead, but will wake again to a healthier life.

On Plate III., I give two designs for waiters to be worked out in flat chasing. Fig. I. if drawn in full would show three masks, three sprays of oak and laurel leaves and three sets of scrolls and ornaments. The tray may be of any size to suit the taste or require-

PLATE III.

FIG. I.

FIG. II.

ments of the student, and after sticking on the cement, as described in Chapter I., page 4, divided with the spring compasses if large enough, if not the hinge compasses into six equal parts round the outside of the flat part of the waiter marked A at bottom, afterwards drawing a line with the straight edge (a broad piece of crinoline-steel is very good if easily obtained as it lies very flat on the waiter) from point to point which will, of course, give the centre where the lines cross. Strike with the compasses the inside band, and then the outside one which ends in the scroll-heads. First outline the inner band, draw on a section of the ornament enclosed and trace it out as described in Chapter VI., page 48. The tracers best suited will be Nos. 14 and 16, page 17. Take a piece of thin writing paper, place it on the section outlined, and rub on the surface with a lead pencil until the impression is distinct, then perforate it with No. 1 punch, Chapter I. If the student takes a sixth part, viz., from B to A, the paper before rubbing with the pencil should be large enough to cover a third part of the ornament, because he can then double the paper, taking care that he does it evenly, and by perforating when double get a third part of the design, excepting the oak and laurel sprays, which cannot be obtained by the same means. The student will have the laurel spray upon his rubbing, but not the oak; so that, if when the paper is perforated he or she will cut the paper the exact size to fit in the band, and before unfolding it reverse the paper on the tray, pounce over the pattern with a small pounce bag, filled with whiting, as described in another chapter, and illustrated on page 3 with the other implements, another sixth part can be traced out with the omission of the oak spray; the paper should then be unfolded and the spray omitted drawn in the space on the paper left for it and perforated. The student will then have a complete section of one-third of the whole design, which he can pounce on in the way the sixth part was done, and get another third; and again another pouncing will make another third, and complete the design. In the professional workshop it is customary to work from the dotted outline left by the pounced whiting, but it is the safer plan to scriber it on with the point (No. 1), as the dust may then be wiped off, and all fear of erasing the design removed. But when outlined from the pounce, the fingers are not permitted to touch the metal, otherwise they would, of course, obliterate the design. If a third of the design is drawn on by the student, viz., from B to B, a single thickness of paper would only be required to be perforated instead of a doubled one as described. When the outline is completed, the ground may be matted with a dead mat, as indicated in the blackened part of design, and the ornament simply veined, left plain, or matted with worn grain mats, as a contrast to the ground, or the ornament be matted with varied mats, and the ground left bright or plain, as indicated in Fig. I. Plate III.

Fig. II. Plate III. is another design for flat chasing another tray which, as the former one, may be made any size and worked in exactly the same way. The alternate panels of wild roses and michaelmas daisies should have the ground work in them done with a dot (as shown) or different mat to the panels in black. On the ground here and on Fig. I. may be sawn away—with a fret-saw as described in last chapter—if the ornament is extended so as to form "ties" to the bands which enclose it (see illustration page 106).

Again, Fig. I. on Plate IV. is an arrangement of the acanthus, and musk blossom, and foliage, showing a plain ground and matted ornament. The flowers should be matted with a different tool to the foliage,

PLATE IV.

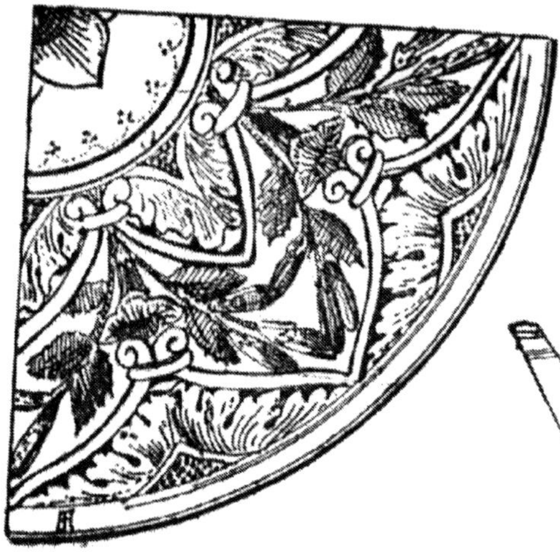

FIG. I.

FIG. II.

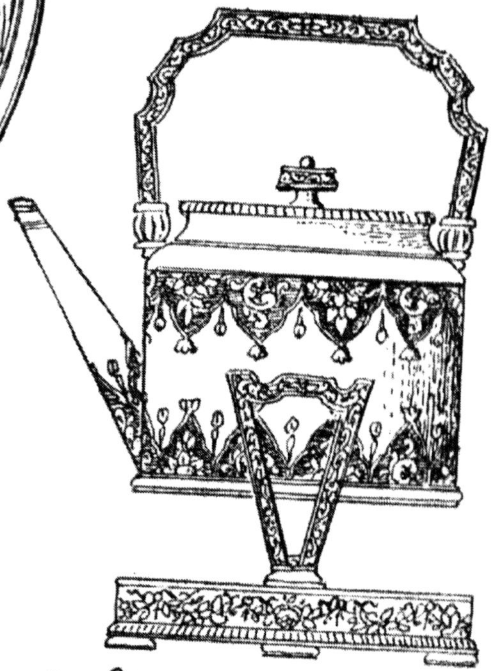

FIG. III.

FIG. IV.

and even the leaves would show to advantage if varied with streaky and dead, or soft-mixed mats. The acanthus arrangement that occupies the other panels should be done with another mat, a grain mat, or shaded carefully with a tracer. The design may be marked on in exactly the same way as the waiter on Plate III. in sections.

Fig. II. is old in shape, but the ornament is arranged on the body, stand, support, handle and spout to illustrate a simple flat chased design; and all vessels with flat sides—can shaped such as this—or biscuit boxes of perpendicular sides are better suited for flat chasing than repoussé, or embossing, because the shape does not bind the metal as in globular forms, and if raised with the snarl it will be found to lift up beyond the parts desired, the flat shape not giving sufficient resistance to the part the snarl does not touch—the metal round the ornament. The handle, too, in such an article would invariably be hollow, but the metal of such a thickness, and the space so slight between the bottom, top and sides, that it will bear the impression of the chasing tools lightly treated without giving way. This, of course, would also apply to the support on which the kettle hangs, but the stand would require filling with cement, and stuck upon a block. "a" and b are enlarged details of the ornament given to the panels on the kettle.

Fig. III. is part of a flute and ornament enclosed without any matting whatever. It is from a set well-known in the silver and electro plate world, as the Abercorn, said originally to have been designed by the Duke of Abercorn. The broad lines are intended to show the hollow flute, and the diaper work is accomplished with a straight tracer, round and oval dots, such as Nos. 2, 15, and 19, Chapters I. and III.

Fig. IV. is another design showing the ornament when left quite plain, and the ground dead-matted; or by strengthening—making broader the ornament—the ground shown in black may be perforated with a fret-saw, and a pleasant result thereby gained, as shown by "tying" or joining the ornament to the outer band, see the parts marked B in section of Fig. A given below, and which appears as a whole on Plate, page 101.

FIG. A.

CHAPTER XII.

FLAT CHASING AND CARVING, PLATED TABLE CUTLERY AND JEWELLERY.

It will be observed that the articles chosen in the previous chapter to illustrate Flat Chasing are all wrought out of sheet metal. That is, metal which has been reduced from a cast ingot of an inch or an inch and a half in thickness, to the gauge and width required in the sheet. It is then annealed, spun, stamped, or hammered by hand (whichever process may be best suited) into the shapes required; but in the case of jewellery, the articles are frequently cast or solid, or, if hollow, are so minute that they necessitate quite a different treatment, e.g., the finger rings (for which, I am indebted to Mr. Mayell, Gold Ring Maker, of Clerkenwell, London; and Unett Street, Birmingham). With very few exceptions the rings are made out of thick wire rounded on the front side and flat, or nearly so, on the inner side, as shown, most conspicuously, by the shapes A, G, and K in the illustration on Plate V.; some cast in flat strips varying in size from one and a half to two and a half inches long, and others, such as B, L, M, N, and O, cut into strips out of thick sheet. The strips are sent in this condition to the Assay Hall, the standard of gold tested and marked 9, 15, 18, or 22 carat, according to the quality. They are then bent so as to bring the two ends together, which are securely attached by solder and afterwards boiled in diluted aquafortis in a thick copper vessel made specially for the purpose. This process cleanses the gold, removing the blackened coating caused by heating pot and the borax used in soldering. They are then rounded on a tapered mandrel with a mallet, and any unevenness of seams made by the soldering of the two ends of strips removed by the hammer and file. They are now ready for decoration, and are passed over to the chaser for that purpose. Some are outlined and shaded by the engraver, and matted between the ornament by the chaser, but the greater portion are chased. It has been a custom, too, by makers of inferior gold rings of this class to those illustrated here, to obtain effective designs from the chaser, executed on an assortment of rings, and copying them as nearly as practicable by means of rolling or stamping, which are purely mechanical processes; and to make the imitation more complete and more difficult for the purchaser to recognize, they are sometimes repaired in parts by the engraver's graver or chaser's mat. When a design has its ornament repeated at equal distances, it should first be divided into the number of sections it is intended to form: K should be divided into four, L into ten, M into six, N into eight, R into ten, and so on. If the rings are solid, they are chased on a very slightly tapered mandrel separately, but often the chaser sticks a row of seven or eight on a bowl block, which is always preferable for solidity, first pressing the cement into each ring with the finger and thumb. The best means of securing the bowl block from shaking is by placing it in the leather ring (see Plate II., page 3). The cement must, of course, be hot, or it will not be pliable, but being rather thick, is not hot enough to burn if used with dexterity. And it is best to roll it in the palms of the hands into a ball the size of a large marble and place it into the ring and press it quickly with the finger and thumb until it becomes flattened at the sides, and the circumference

PLATE V.

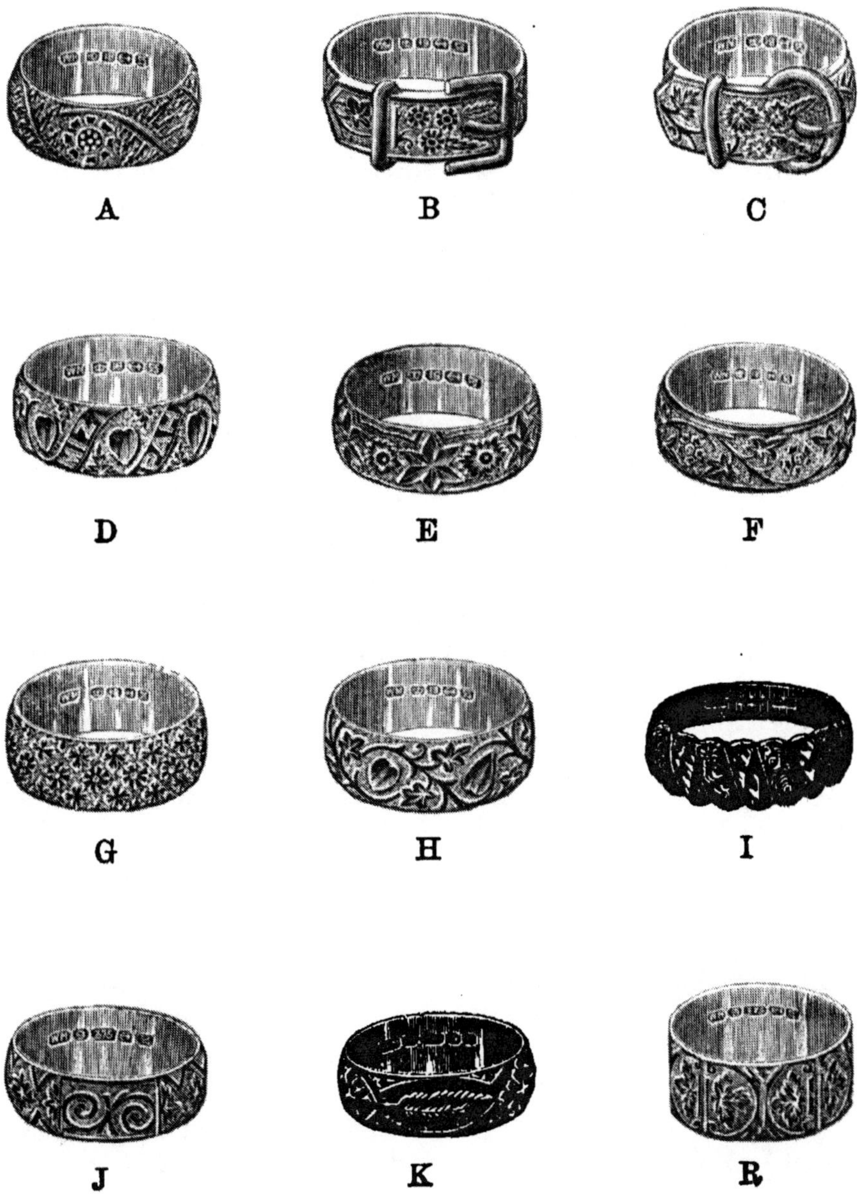

expanding until it touches the inside of the ring all round. The cement on the bowl or basin block (see illustration on Plate II.), which should be thick, made so by a greater proportion of plaster of Paris than pitch, is either placed on a stand or held in the hands before a sharp fire, or melted with a gas flame in the manner explained for releasing work in Chapter I. The fire is always preferable where convenient, as the melting is much more even, and burning the cement never occurring, which is frequently the reverse when melting with a gas flame, unless the greatest care is taken. What I mean by burning the cement is causing dull blisters to rise by the fierce flame of gas, which are as thin embers and which no longer retain the tenacity of the cement in its original condition.

There is another way of sticking the rings on to the block, which is sometimes adopted, viz., by scraping the melted pitch with each ring and pressing it first into one then another until the seven or eight, or number the chaser can conveniently get on the block, are brought close together and made secure—this is usually accomplished for the greater part of the performance with the broad face of the hammer (see illustration, page 6), and the fingers and thumb, but as the cement would be hotter than in the former method the fingers should be moistened with water; professionals invariably apply their fingers to their lips to serve the purpose. When the cement is cold the work is ready for chasing, as explained elsewhere, and supposing we had "A" to chase, we should strike the flower shown on the ring very lightly with a bowl or ring punch the full size, afterwards the centre much harder with a smaller ring tool, the centre stem of the ferns with a slightly curved tracer. A very small straight tracer should then be used to divide into petals the space between the centre bowl punch and outer one, and a very small bent tracer struck twice to shape the end of each petal—the same will serve for the leaflets of the fern, and a straight tracer used for the centre fibre of each a little larger than that used for the petals of the flower. The edges are then "jagged" or "chopped," as it is technically called, with the same small straight tracer, to form the serrations in the leaflets. The groundwork is done with a very small, sharp *French freezer*. Although called French, the best made were by Mr. Parkins, of London, whose splendid mats, grain and mixed, or freezers, all bear his name stamped upon the sides. The ground should be beaten slightly below the ornament, because in this instance the latter is lapped, giving a bright contrast to the dead matting. Let us now take "E." It contains six stars and six flowers. Make the stars first with a small straight tracer, the lines that are parallel to the edges of the ring with the same, then strike with a ring-punch the centres of the flowers between the stars and from the centre six lines radiating from it at equal distances with a very small straight tracer. Use then a small curved tracer for the ends of the petals by joining it to the ends of the short straight lines, making the opposite ends of the curved tracer meet, which will form ovated ends which may be serrated by tilting the small straight tracer and striking the edge of the petal in the direction of the centre. The flower is shaded by moving the straight tracer round the centre (see illustration); another straight tracer whetted to a more obtuse angle (see No. 15, Chap. III.), but one-third the size, should be struck in the six corners of the star rather heavily, and graduated towards the centre, the ground matted with a freezer in the same manner as A. It will be observed that G is decorated with a small kind of diaper or diamond pattern. To insure the diamonds being in rotation, and the same size, a line should be ruled round the centre of the ring from the edge with the spring compasses and divided into half the number of sections that the diamonds occupy round the middle of the ring, that is if there are twelve, divide into six. Or even a readier way—divide into four equal parts, and each part into three, making the twelve; draw a perpendicular line from edge to edge of ring through each division. Make six large diamonds first with a straight tracer, such as No. 15, Chap. III., by passing it obliquely through every other division on the line round the middle of the ring from the top of one of the perpendicular lines touching the edge of the ring on your right hand to the bottom of the third line on your left. Trace the other five lines parallel to it by starting at the top of the perpendicular line that the first traced line touches the bottom of, and so in like manner until the six are traced. Now trace from left to right, in an oblique direction, from the top ends of the lines just made to the bottom crossing in the centre. This will give you the six large diamonds. Now trace parallel lines in the same way from the ends of the lines between the diamonds at the top to those at the bottom, this will give you the twelve diamonds round the centre, twelve with their points touching both edges of the ring, and twelve semi-diamonds at each edge (see illustration G). The lines in this instance that form the diamonds would be done by the professional with a very narrow dead-mat, or a fine corded tool, for the means of contrast. The small flowers and crosses that fill the diamonds would be done with a very small ring tool and straight tracer in the same way as those described in A and E. It will be seen that the ring I is different in shape to those I have just described. The seven rounded sections in front are either cast in the ring or filed by the ring-maker into shape before the chaser applies his ornament. Three of the seven sections are made into small diamonds or facets, by tracing heavily, crosswise, in oblique directions (see illustration) with a tracer like

No. 17, Chap. III., but straight. The lines made with it being broad and clear form each minute diamond into a little pyramid. The chaser, here, too, it may be noted, has for contrast covered the alternate sections with minute scrolls, technically called "nuggeting," which has a dead but very rich effect. Now, the remainder of illustrations, B, C, F, H, J, K, N, and D (on which the "Mizpah" would be either engraved on bands or the letters soldered on before chasing) may all be executed on similar lines to those described; and for this, and nearly the whole of commercial jewellery, chasing is executed with sharp tools—the tracers, with few exceptions, are more like chisels, and the mixed mats or freezers of corresponding sharpness. And all the foregoing may be worked upon mandrels or on a bowl block as described; but should the rings be hollow, as they sometimes are, the chaser must boil them in powdered alum and water; one or two small holes about $\frac{1}{32}$ of an inch in diameter are drilled in the insides for the purpose of admitting the liquid alum when in a boiling state, into the hollow band. A large bladder will rise over the vessel containing the liquid when the water added is exhausted, and the vessel is placed on one side to cool. A copper, brass, or iron vessel will do equally well, and the size in proportion to the number of rings boiled in it. When it is cold it sets into one solid mass, and is broken away from the rings, which should be stuck in cement, to chase. If they are attempted on a mandrel, unless the work is exceedingly light, they will in all probability be damaged, and may burst at the edges, where they are brazed, as the iron is harder and has greater power of resistance than the alum. The majority of small articles, viz:—ornaments for watch-chains, etc., that cannot be conveniently filled with cement, are made sound for chasing in this way (see illustrations L, M, N, O, P, and Q). When the chasing is finished, they are again put into water and the alum boiled out of them. Should the article be unsound in any part when the work is commenced, it will sink into a hollow so soon as touched by the punch, and the worker should immediately cease to work on that part, but do as much

L

M

N

as is quite solid, and when completed, boil the alum out with the others, and refill, as described, by boiling again in alum. The whole of the foregoing rings and slides are simply of commercial average—but I have chosen them here as a means of best illustrating flat chasing on jewellery. There is another kind of ornamenta-

O

P

Q

tion however, which, while dealing with the subject of rings, I may mention here. That is carving. It is not, however, entirely confined to rings, as keys and lock furniture in steel, the ornamentation on fire-arms, gun and pistol locks, and the decoration on the stocks is often of this kind; and although the ornament is often rather flat on the surface as in the case of the fruit or christening spoon handle (see Fig. I., page 117), it is the result of quite different means to that hitherto described, viz. :—beating away the ground-work to give the ornament a degree of relief. As in the finger rings A to B, page 109, and the ornament for watch chains L, M, N, O, P, Q, page 114, on such as L, M, and Q, the ground is frequently beaten below the ornament, but in O, P, and N, the deep incisions made by the tracers and the shading usually give the required effect without beating away. It will be observed that the one marked P is the only one that would admit well of such a process, there being no large spaces of ground on the other two, but the whole surface covered with minute

ornament, the one consisting of a kind of small daisy, which is obtained by striking a sharp corded bowl, or ring-tool all over the ball, making each ring fit as closely as possible to the one last struck; a minute bowl-punch is struck in the centre of each larger ring, and a small straight tracer struck eight or nine times—being tilted from the centre—to form the petals. All the punches for this class of work should, like those used on the keeper-rings spoken of, be very acute.

But the signet rings R, S, U, V and W, are intended for carved patterns, and therefore for the first outline of the ornament tools with blunter faces (see 14, 15, 16, and 17, page 17, Chap. III.) should be used—but owing to the smallness of the work, the punches should, of course, be proportionately small. When the design is outlined, small chisels should be used such as the one illustrated in Chap. X., page 94, for piercing purposes—straight or curved as the work may require. We will take the ring R, when the design has been "scribered" — scratched on with a pointed punch (see No. 1, page 1) on both shoulders of the ring—secure the ring in the cement on a bowl or basin block with the one side facing you as drawn. Take a small tracer, the shape of 14, Chap. III. p. 17, and trace round the part intended to receive the stone—round the head of the cherub, next the wings. Lay the tracer aside for a moment and take a small straight tracer down each

V

W

side from under each wing, to the bottom semi-rosette under the head. Take up the curved tracer again or one bent rather more—such as 17, illustrated on same page—and outline the semi-rosette with it. Now apply the chisels, chipping or carving away the ground to leave the ornament in relief. A small tracer still more curved than the other two should be used for the hair, and the parts of the wings nearest the head. For the longer feathers of the wings the tracer that outlined them may be used. A very small straight tracer should be used for the divisions in the rosettes, and a minute ring punch for centres. A rough form having thus been acquired, a small fine riffle should be first applied to remove any sharp bur, and lastly, small planishers for the face and wings —striking an oval one in the inner corners of the eyes and carrying it down the sides of the nose, and under the nostrils and nether lip. The other designs may be worked out in the same way.

The spoon handle, Fig. I., from the top to the husk marked a at the commencement of bowl may be treated in exactly the same way; but the ground indicated by the blackened part will much more readily be made quite even by matting, after it has been carved out with the small chisels. The ornament in the bowl is intended for repoussé, as the metal here would be too thin to carve.

The last class of chasing left to deal with is that of dessert cutlery (see illustrations 1, 2, 3, and 4, page 118). The most expensive and durable is the "close plated," that is, the knives are steel and plated with sheet silver. The knife is immersed into a vessel of molten soft solder (a mixture of tin and lead). A strip of thin sheet silver, rather longer and broader than the blade, is laid first on one side and burnished over with a heated bevelled oblong soldering iron until any crease or uneven part is removed. The surplus silver is then cut away with scissors or snips and the other side treated the

FIG. I

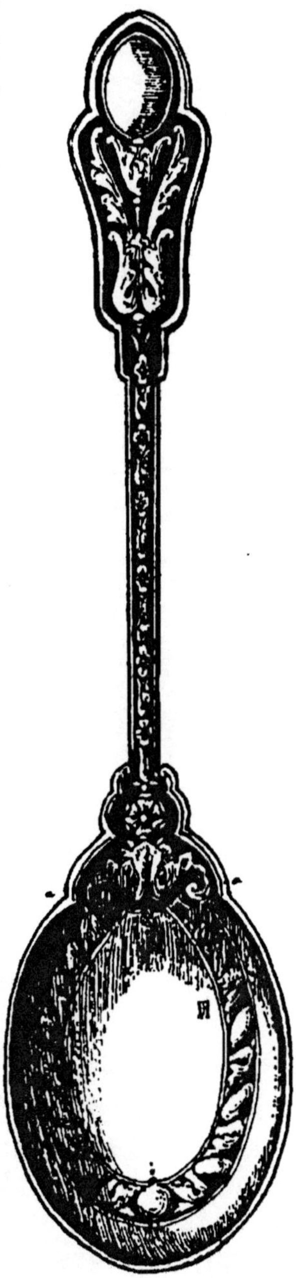

same. The edges of the two strips meet at the back, the edge, and top and bottom—or bolster of the blade near the handle—is fixed. Any surplus solder that may have escaped and got on to the surface is smoothed off with fine or worn smooths (files). The blade

is then polished with lime on leather bobs—a wooden wheel faced with leather—and is ready for the chaser. The extent the chaser can go in this particular class of work is extremely limited, owing to the nature of material he has to deal with. And when he first attempts it, although proficient in other kinds of work, he is often defeated in his first attempts at success, unless he is fortunate enough to have the secrets laid open to him by some one who has had experience. For instance, if the tools are similar to those used for jewellery, very acute, they immediately cut through the silver and make a mere scratch, as it were, for an outline—if very blunt, as used for figure work, the outline is not sufficiently defined; therefore the worker requires them to be whetted to an angle, but like those on page 17, Chap. III. Again the mats are as important as the tracers, the finest are required, or if coarse, they must not be sharp, if they are, the space cannot be deadened successfully; and in an attempt to go over the same ground many times, the silver plate is removed in patches and the solder clogs the mats. Therefore very fine streaky mats and dead mats are the most used. Small blunt bowl punches and corded punches are also introduced with great advantage; and perhaps the punch in greatest demand upon this work is the single pick, whetted in a pyramidically shaped way. It is used for the tendrils of vines, running round the backs of scrolls as in Fig. IV., serpentine lines on dead ground as shown in Fig. VI., page 32, graduated dots, as in Fig. III., page 118, and, indeed, it makes so great a show that where the chaser can introduce it, the opportunity is seldom lost. This class of work should be done very lightly throughout, and the same surface must not be worked over too many times, or the silver will be removed as stated above, and, of course, the article spoiled. A gas flame *must never* be applied to release it from the cement. If it is, the sudden and fierce heat will blister up the silver in an instant and make a sorry sight of the article. The work should be placed in front of a sharp fire until the cement round it becomes melted (thick cement should be used, i.e. two-thirds plaster of Paris, one of pitch), and if the blades are slightly greased before sticking on, they will leave—by pushing or pulling them sideways—the cement with only the dirty coating of oil made so by its adhesion to the pitch, which a little turps or cleansing fluid, and the application of fine box saw-dust will entirely remove.

CHAPTER XIII.

FLUTING.

THESE last few years have witnessed a very powerful revival of the very beautiful branch of decoration known as fluting, which was practised by the goldsmiths of the sixteenth century with such marked success, and which—in the present century—up to the first half, was not infrequently recognized as a distinct calling in the silversmith's art, although many of the best workers who hammered up the shapes could flute them too; but latterly it has become almost exclusively a part of the profession of the worker in repoussé. Owing, as I take it, to the greater mastery over the punches, he is enabled to obtain the same result in very much less time.

There are many very graceful specimens of this class of work; and the tall covered goblet (see Fig. I., Plate VI., page 122) is one of several similar in shape that were executed in the sixteenth century. The globular forms on the cover, and foot, if raised—which I should think they would be—after the cup was made into the first graceful form, would be executed with a punch as large as the globular forms on the cup, and shaped as No. 5, illustrated in Chap. I., page 1, struck from the inside while the opposite or front side would be laid on wax or cement—or with the snarl, as those on the body would have to be raised; but this could only bring them into

PLATE VI.

FIG. I.

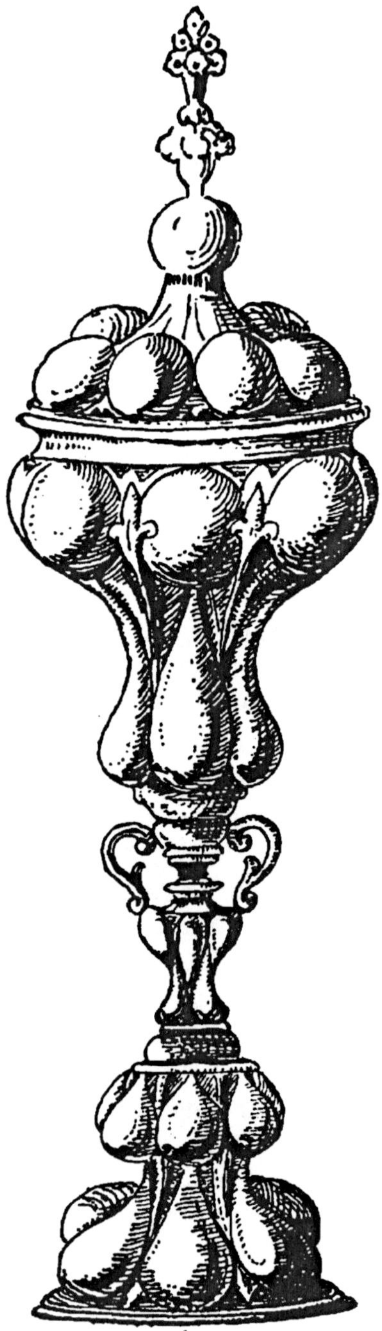

rough form, so that they would require to be modelled into finished shapes by such a punch as No. VI., given in those below, when filled with cement. The snarling iron, too, should be a very large one—not necessarily so large as the ornament, but two-thirds at least. Soft cement should be used to fill the cup with, and when nearly cold, a curved punch with a face similar to the straight ones. Nos. II. and III., illustrated below, should be used for outlining the globular forms referred

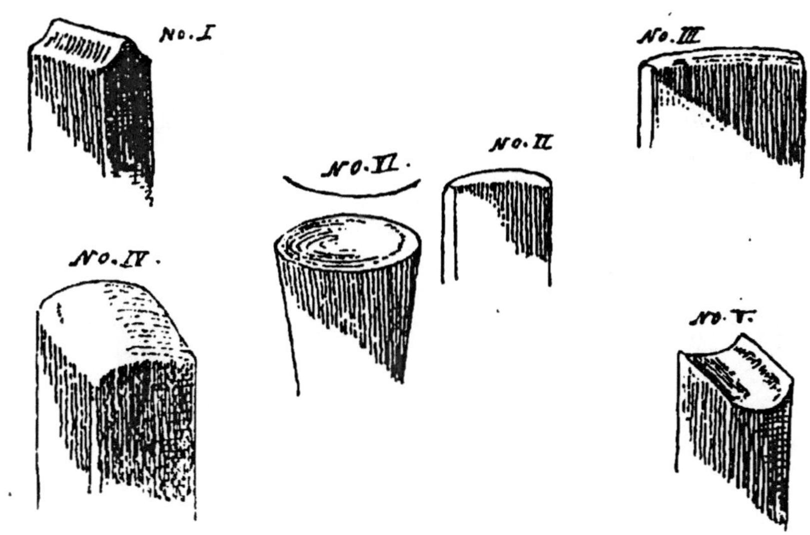

to above, and No. II. for the flutes that extend from them at the top of the body of the cup to those at the bottom. The metal will, in most instances, when the pitch is soft, rise between the lines made by the tool, so evenly that planishing is not necessary; when it is, a punch the shape of No. V., but receding at the two ends of the hollow, or groove, and with no sharp edges, will smooth the uneven parts. Or in place of No. II. to make the lines, a tool shaped on the sides of the end—like No. I., but higher in the centre as shown in No. II., instead of straight. When the fluting is finished the chasing or repoussé ornament may be executed in the manner described in other chapters.

Fig. II., page 124, is intended for an alms or rosewater dish; the size may be determined by the student, but 12in. and 14in. in diameter are the most general sizes in alms dishes, but lady students in the Birmingham Municipal School of Art have made, and

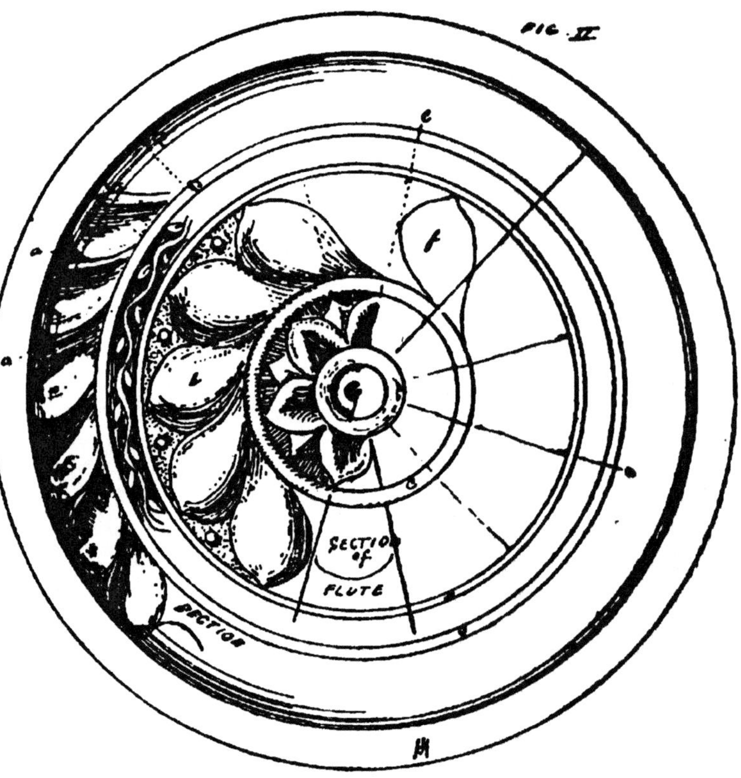

ornamented very successfully, several rosewater dishes 18in. and 20in. in diameter under the able tuition of Mr. Frank G. Jackson, who is Principal in Ornament there.

Supposing we had the ornamenting of the dish (Fig. II.) to do, we should first strike the bands C, D, C, from the centre and divide the outer band into four equal parts, e to e, and each fourth part into three, making twelve divisions in all. From the twelve divisions then rule lines to the centre from the outer line e, and draw the raised flutes as shown in "f;" afterwards stick it on to the cement and first strike the small band that forms the centre of rosette with two ring tools—in case we had not one so large as the outer line, trace it with a punch like No. 16 (see page 17). The three outer bands, c, d, and c, with No. 14 punch, and with the same two punches the six sections of rosette, the raised flutes, and round the ends of the hollow flutes (see "a" to "a")—if we had marked them on the front first. The small beads between the raised flutes with a ring punch. It would then be ready for reversing, and the impression of the outline would enable us to see the portion to be raised. We should draw straight lines, as "G" to "G," from the points made by the traced lines on the front from "a" to "a" and "a" to h, drawing the curved lines of the hollow flute on the back as we had drawn them for the raised flute, shown in "f," on the front. And working on the back, our best tool for this purpose would be No. I., page 123; such a punch as No. "26" on page 63 we should use to shape the hollow flute from the back, and beat up the raised flute with No. IV., page 123. This we should do on a sand bag or wax to get a fair degree of height, and thereby shorten the labour before filling it with cement. When in the cement, we should finish the flutes with the same punches used on the sand bag or wax. The centre of rosette No. 4 punch, page 1, and the band round it forming the outer part of the centre with No. 11, page 1, and No. II. in this chapter. We should raise the sections of rosette, beads, and laurel as described on pages 14 and 15 for similar work. We should then take it again from the cement, clean it in the manner spoken of on page 9, and stick it on the cement to finish on the front with planishers, as in Fig. I, page 122.

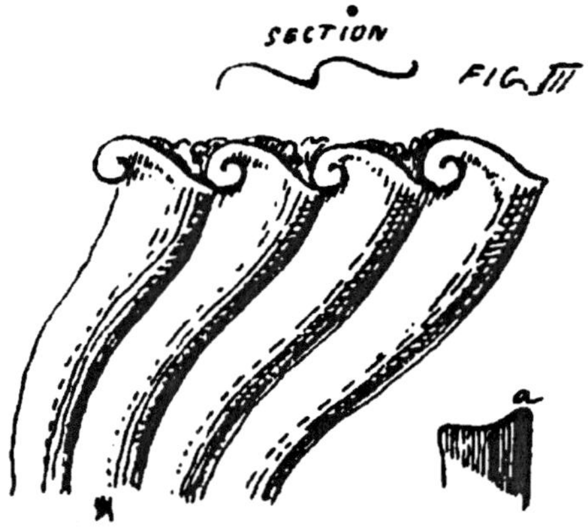

In Fig. III. a curved flute terminating with a scroll should be worked with a punch shaped on the end as

the section drawn beside it, and the end marked "a" used for the sunken part of the flute shown in shadow.

Fig. IV. is an old kind of flute known as the "quill," which would be principally executed with punches shaped similarly to No. IV. in this chapter.

In Fig V. are given several kinds of curved flutes, showing how they may be varied. The first on the left

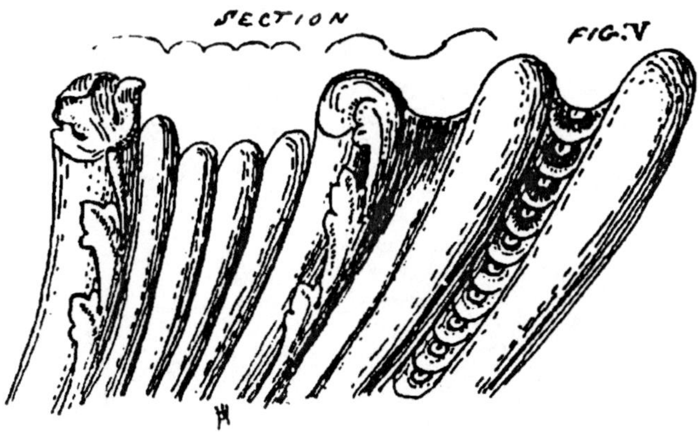

side is a large raised flute with husk ending, and four smaller or "finger" flutes following; the next, a large flute with an acanthus scroll ending, followed by a hollow flute, and adjoining that a plain, large flute

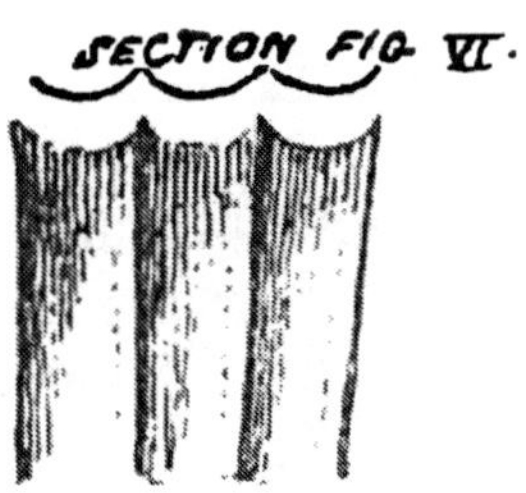

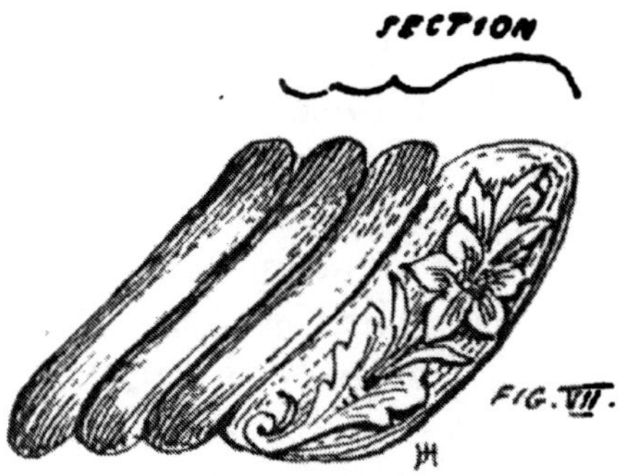

with a hollow flute worked out into ornament. All ornament on flutes should be raised above the flutes, to give it the appearance of having been laid on them. Fig. VI. is intended for a straight hollow flute and can be executed with a smaller tool but of similar shape to

No. IV. on page 123 of this chapter. Fig. VII. is for an alternate arrangement of three hollow flutes, and one large full or raised flute with floral decoration. Fig. VIII. is drawn to show the student the simplest method of drawing on the flutes when curved. When the article has been divided into the number of flutes required, straight lines should be drawn as shown in the dotted lines on this Figure. After the perpendicular lines are drawn, horizontal ones should be ruled as shown in "C" and B, and the curves drawn through the intersections, from the top of the straight line to the

FIG. VIII.

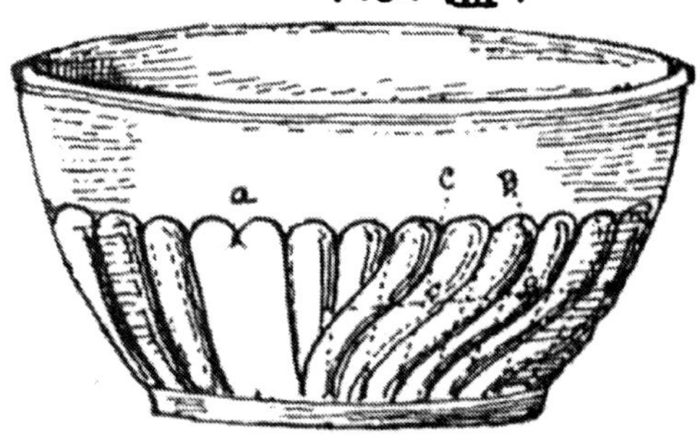

bottom of the adjoining or next but one, as the curvature of the flute may determine.

All curved flutes should be marked on in this way and the tops or rounded ends traced first. It is preferable in some instances, though not absolutely necessary, to outline each alternate flute (see the part marked "a"). In nearly all instances, too, where the flutes are in high relief on vessels such as Fig. VIII., cups and articles similarly constructed, a snarling iron is used, and for such work as Figs. V. and VIII., an oval-shaped end will be found preferable to a rounded one—being better adapted to the shape of the flute, it will enable the worker to obtain a much more even surface. In such a shape as the teapot (Fig. IV.), and the scroll-

K

ending flute Fig. III., the parts in relief are obtained by heating down the other parts of the metal into hollows, as shown by those portions in shadow.

In Fig. IX. are given two examples of hollow fluting with graduated beads raised in each alternate twisted flute, and an acanthus leaf in each alternate straight one.

Fluting may be varied to an almost unlimited extent, and the student must bear this in mind, that the few

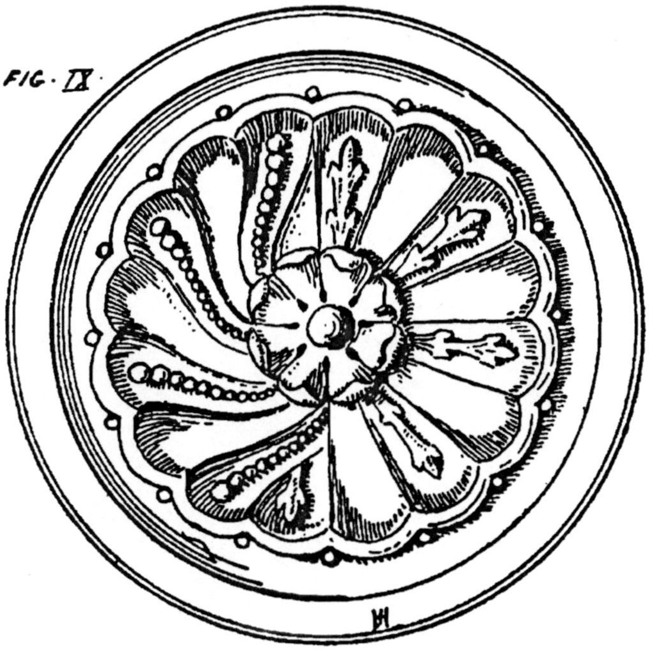

FIG. IX.

specimens I give here have been chosen with a view to convey an idea to the student how he or she may best begin the work of fluting generally.

A word respecting pewter wares, before closing the book, may be said here. One of the most beautiful specimens is the famous ewer by François Briot, an artist of the sixteenth century. It is embellished with winged horses, figures, and masks, and has been extensively copied in metal casting and pottery. It cannot, however, be looked upon as repoussé in the present acceptation of the term—as the ornament has been acquired by beating the metal into brass moulds or dies. The pewter dishes in South Kensington Museum may mislead the student, if not acquainted with this means by which the effect has been obtained. For my own choice I do not like pewter to ornament with repoussé—it is too soft; but well suited for beating into moulds of harder metal, as in Briot's works.

Etching, engraving, enamelling, damascening, niello, and modelling are intended for another volume.

GILBERT AND RIVINGTON, LD., ST. JOHN'S HOUSE, CLERKENWELL, E.C.

J. J. WRIGHT.

THE SCULPTOR AND ART STUDENT'S GUIDE to the Proportions of the Human Form, with Measurements in feet and inches of Full-grown Figures of Both Sexes and of Various Ages. Translated by J. J. WRIGHT. Plates reproduced by J. SUTCLIFFE. Oblong Folio, 31*s*. 6*d*.

G. REDGRAVE.

OUTLINES OF HISTORIC ORNAMENT. By G. REDGRAVE. Translated from the German. Edited by G. REDGRAVE. Crown 8vo. 4*s*.

R. N. WORNUM.

THE CHARACTERISTICS OF STYLES: An Introduction to the Study of the History of Ornamental Art. By R. N. WORNUM. Ninth Edition. Royal 8vo. 8*s*.

G. PERROT, and C. CHIPIEZ.

A HISTORY OF ANCIENT ART IN PHŒNICIA, CYPRUS, AND ASIA MINOR. 500 Illustrations. 2 vols. Imperial 8vo. 42*s*.

A HISTORY OF ART IN ANCIENT EGYPT. With 616 Illustrations. 2 vols. Imperial 8vo. 42*s*.

A HISTORY OF ART IN CHALDÆA AND ASSYRIA. With 452 Illustrations. 2 vols. Imperial 8vo. 42*s*.

A HISTORY OF ANCIENT ART IN SARDINIA, JUDÆA, SYRIA, AND ASIA MINOR. With 395 Illustrations. 2 vols. Imperial 8vo. 36*s*.

A HISTORY OF ANCIENT ART IN PERSIA. With 254 Illustrations, and 12 Steel and Coloured Plates. Imperial 8vo. 21*s*.

A HISTORY OF ANCIENT ART IN PHRYGIA—LYDIA, and CARIA—LYCIA. With 280 Illustrations. Imperial 8vo. 15*s*.

SYLLABUS OF ART EXAMINATIONS.

Minute of Science and Art Department of April 12th, 1892.

MODEL DRAWING,

ELEMENTARY AND ADVANCED STAGES.

MESSRS. CHAPMAN & HALL beg to announce that they are now prepared to supply the Models and Vases prescribed by the Science and Art Department for the use at the above Art Examinations. These Models and Vases have been manufactured to their Special Order, and have been duly Approved by the Authorities.

The Entire Collection consists of—

(1) Vase—Bottle from the Three Regular Objects of Form.
(2) Vase—from the Set of Fine Majolica Vases.
(3) Vase—from the Set of Three Earthenware Vases.
(4) Cube—Large.
(5) Cube—Small.
(6) Cone.
(7) Cylinder.
(8) Hexagonal Prism.
(9) Triangular Prism.
(10) Square Prism.
(11) Square Pyramid.
(12) Skeleton Cube.
(13) Sphere.
(14) Ring.

PRICE IN BOX :—

Set for Elementary Stage (Subject 3A—First Figure, 2*l.* 16*s.* net; Set for Advanced Stage (Subject 3A—Second Figure), 1*l.* 4*s.* net; Complete Set, 4*l.* net.

PRICES OF SEPARATE MODELS, &c., as under:—

No. 1, 5*s.* 6*d.*; No. 2, 8*s.* 6*d.*; No. 3, 6*s.*; Nos. 4, 6, 7, 8, 11, 12, and 13, 6*s.* 8*d.* each; Nos. 9 and 10, 5*s.* 6*d.* each; Nos. 5 and 14, 3*s.* each, net.*

* *Packing will be charged as an extra item.*

MODELS AND VASES.

ONE WIRE QUADRANGLE, 14 inches square, with a Circle and Cross within it, and one Straight Wire; one Skeleton Wire Cube, 11 inches high; three Wire Models; one Sphere; one Cone, 18 inches high; one Cylinder, 12 inches high; one Hexagonal Prism, 15 inches high; one Solid Cube, 10 inches high; Skeleton Cube, 10 inches. Set complete, 2*l.* 5*s.* 6*d.*

INTERMEDIATE DRAWING MODELS. Contains Twelve well-finished Models; average height, 8 inches. Including Stand, in box, 30*s.*

THE 'HANDY' SET OF CO-ORDINATE PLANES AND TEN MODELS. In Box complete, 10*s.* net.

J. M. DICKSEE'S CONSTRUCTIVE SOLID DRAWING MODELS. 34 pieces. In Box, 8*l.*

WISE'S ELEMENTARY DRAWING MODELS in Box. With Stand, 4*l.*; without Stand, 3*l.*

SCHOOL DRAWING MODELS. Set of 17 Large Models, 3*l.* net.

BOX OF SMALL MODELS, average size 7 inches, 1*l.* 4*s.* net.

DAVIDSON'S SOLID MODELS, in Box, 2*l.*

FIVE SELECTED VASES IN MAJOLICA WARE, 2*l.* 11*s.*

THREE SELECTED VASES in EARTHEN-WARE, 18*s.*

THREE OBJECTS of *FORM* in POTTERY, 18*s.* 6*d.*

A NEW SET OF THREE VASES, 18*s.*

MILLER'S SECTIONAL MODELS for the EASIER TEACHING of SOLID GEOMETRY. Complete in Box, 7*l.* 10*s.*

DAVIDSON'S ADVANCED DRAWING MODELS, 9*l.*

Copies for Outline Drawing.

LARGE FREEHAND EXAMPLES FOR CLASS TEACHING. Specially prepared under the authority of the Science and Art Department. Six Sheets. Size 60 by 40 inches. 9*s.* Mounted on rollers, 27*s.*

DRAWING BOOK OF THE GOVERNMENT SCHOOL OF DESIGN, 50 Plates, mounted back and front, 18*s.*; unmounted, sewed, 5*s.*

DRAWING BOOK OF THE GOVERNMENT SCHOOL OF DESIGN. Plates I. to XXII., containing 97 Examples, adapted as Examples for Practice of Standards I. to IV. Small folio, sewed, 2*s.* 6*d.*

ONE SET OF A SELECTION FROM DRAWING BOOK OF THE GOVERNMENT SCHOOL OF DESIGN, 15 Plates, mounted, 6*s.* 6*d.*; unmounted, 1*s.* 6*d.*

WEITBRICHT'S OUTLINES OF ORNAMENT, 12 Plates mounted back and front, 8*s.* 6*d.*; unmounted, 2*s.*

MORGEN'S OUTLINES OF THE HUMAN FIGURE, 20 Plates mounted back and front, 15*s.*; unmounted, 3*s.* 4*d.*

OUTLINES OF TARSIA 4 Plates mounted, 3*s.* 6*d.*; unmounted, 7*d.*

ALBERTOLLI'S FOLIAGE, 4 Plates mounted, 3*s.* 6*d.*; unmounted, 5*d.*

YULE'S FREEHAND DRAWING CARDS.
FIRST GRADE, 5 Sets of 24 Cards. 1*s.* set.
SECOND GRADE, 5 Sets of 12 Cards, 1*s.* set.

GRAMMATIK DER ORNAMENTE. By E. JACOBSTHAL. In 7 Parts of 20 Plates each. Unmounted £3 13*s.* 6*d.*; mounted on cardboard, £11 4*s.* The Parts can be had separately.

OUTLINE OF TRAJAN FRIEZE, mounted, 1*s.*

WALLIS'S DRAWING BOOK, mounted, 8*s.*; unmounted, 3*s.* 6*d.*

OUTLINE DRAWINGS OF FLOWERS, 8 Sheets, mounted, 3*s.* 6*d.*; unmounted, 8*d.*

RENAISSANCE ORNAMENT. Art School Series, by I. P. FRAZER.
Twelve Examples, Book No. 1, 3*d.*
Twelve Examples, Book No. 2, 3*d.*, Cards 6*d.*

GILMOUR & DEAN'S DRAWING BOOKS. Adapted to the Course of Instruction in Drawing as a Class Subject. Eleven Books, 2*d.* each.

COPIES FOR SHADED DRAWING.

COURSE OF DESIGN. By CH. BARGUE. 20 Selected Sheets, £2 9*s.*

ARCHITECTURAL STUDIES. By J. B. TRIPON. 10 Plates, £1.

FOLIATED SCROLL FROM THE VATICAN, unmounted 5*d.*; mounted, 1*s.* 3*d.*

TWELVE HEADS after Holbein, Half-imperial, 36*s.*

DIAGRAM OF COLOUR, unmounted, 9*d.*; mounted, 1*s.* 6*d.*

COTMAN'S PENCIL LANDSCAPES (set of 9), mounted, 15*s.*

" SEPIA DRAWINGS (set of 5), mounted, £1.

ALLONGE'S LANDSCAPES IN CHARCOAL (set of 6), £1 4*s.*, or 4*s.* each.

DIAGRAM OF COLOURS OF THE SPECTRUM, with Explanatory Letterpress, on roller, 5*s.*

RADDE'S COLOUR SCALE, 42 Colours in about 900 shades, in case, £1.

VAN DYCK'S DRAWINGS (set of 9), 12*s.* net.

RELIEF ORNAMENT. Italian Renaissance.

TWENTY	PHOTOGRAPHS—	The Certosa of Pavia, £1 2*s.* net.
NINETEEN	"	John of Bologna, £1 1*s.* 6*d.* net.
THIRTEEN	"	Cathedral of Milan, 15*s.* net.
TWELVE	"	Figures, Certosa of Pavia, 15*s.* net.
ELEVEN	"	Details, Certosa of Pavia, 15*s.* net.
"	"	Pilasters, Certosa of Pavia, 15*s.* net.
TWELVE	"	Details from Venice, 4 vols., each 15*s.* net.
"	"	Capitals and other Details, 15*s.* net.
"	"	Selected Panels, 15*s.* net.
"	"	Selected Details, 15*s.* net.

DRAWINGS in LIGHT and SHADE from CASTS of ORNAMENTS.

By J. E. CHEESE, A.C.T.

Set of 12 Examples, 6*s.* net. Single Copies, 9*d.* net.

DRAWING EXAMPLES.

BY

E. R. TAYLOR,

Head Master, Municipal School of Art, Birmingham.

GEOMETRIC FORMS, LETTERS, AND ORNAMENTS, 28 in number, cut out of Thick Cardboard for tracing round, &c. To be used in the *youngest* Classes of Infant Schools. 3*s*.

A SET OF TWO DRAWING BOOKS, containing Examples (with space for copies by the pupils) as First Exercises on squared paper, for use in Infant Schools and as first preparation for Standards I. and II. 4*d*. per Book.

FREEHAND EXAMPLES on 60 Cards, 7 by 5 ins., gradated up to the 7th Standard and the 2nd Grade Examination. 5*s*.

ENLARGED DIAGRAMS. Freehand Examples on 60 Cards, 21 ins. by 15 ins., gradated up to the 7th Standard and the 2nd Grade Examination, for the collective teaching of large Classes. Explanatory Diagrams are shown for the Teacher's guidance, but so small or light as not to be seen by the Class.

These Examples being on Cardboard have two advantages over books of large Diagrams—viz., any number may be used at the same time in different Classes, and the Example is presented to the Class on a perfectly even surface.

Many of the Examples are displayed by ground or pattern being flat tinted with lines of open texture. The Example is thus better seen by the Class, training is given in judging contrasts of masses, and exercises are provided which will prove useful in light and shade, &c.

Two Parts—Elementary Set of 30, 9*s*. Advanced Set of 30, 9*s*. Complete, 18*s*.

Charts for Model Drawing,

BY

T. C. BARFIELD.

Master of the Art Classes at the Hinckley Grammar School, and formerly Second Master of the Leicester School of Art.

10 *Imperial Sheets*, 8*s*.

Mounted on rollers, varnished, 18*s*.; *on linen only*, 17*s*.

London: CHAPMAN & HALL, LD., Henrietta Street, Covent Garden.

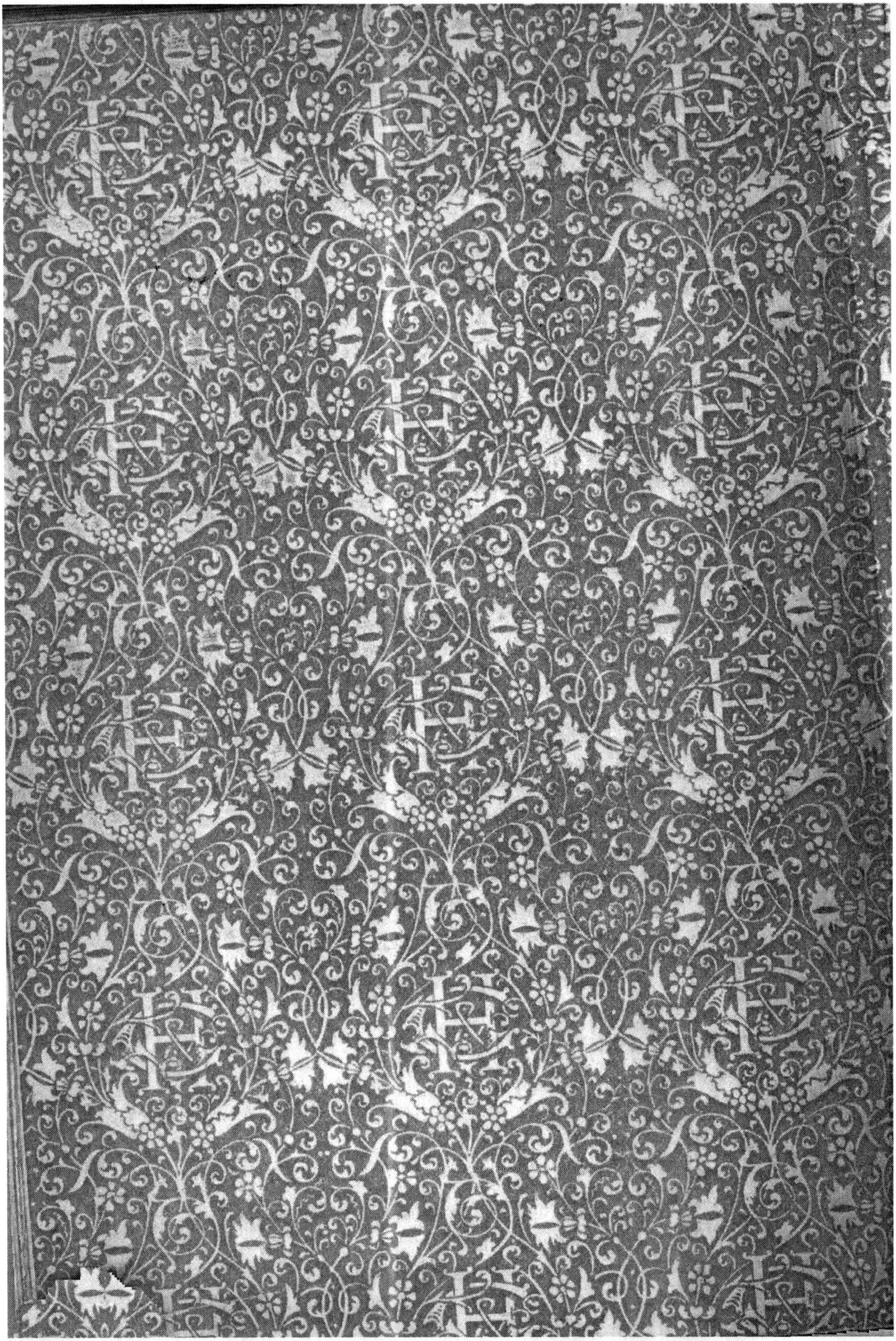

CPSIA information can be obtained at www.ICGtesting.com
Printed in the USA
LVOW110015300513

335950LV00005B/259/P

9 781278 096506